# Attachment Style

The Guide to Strengthening Understanding and Relationships in Your Life. Emotional Intelligence is a Powerful Tool for Finding and Keeping Love

*by*

**Stewart W. Hanton**

# Disclaimer Notice

Please note the information contained within this document is for educational and entertainment purposes only. All effort has been executed to present accurate, up-to-date, and reliable, complete information. No warranties of any kind are declared or implied. Readers acknowledge that the author is not engaging in the rendering of legal, financial, medical, or professional advice. The content within this book has been derived from various sources. Please consult a licensed professional before attempting any techniques outlined in this book.

By reading this document, the reader agrees that under no circumstances is the author responsible for any losses, direct or indirect, which are incurred as a result of the use of the information contained within this document, including, but not limited to, — errors, omissions, or inaccuracies.

© **Copyright 2020 - All rights reserved.**

The content contained within this book may not be reproduced, duplicated, or transmitted without direct written permission from the author or the publisher.

Under no circumstances will any blame or legal responsibility be held against the publisher, or author, for any damages, reparation, or monetary loss due to the information contained within this book. Either directly or indirectly. You are responsible for your own choices, actions, and results.

# Table of Contents

*Introduction* — 8

*Basics of Attachment Theory* — 12

    What Is Attachment Theory? — 14

    Types of Attachment Styles — 15

    Uses of Attachment Theory — 24

    Finding Your Attachment Style — 30

*Dealing with Different Personalities* — 39

    The Pleaser — 41

    The Avoider — 45

    The Vacillator — 49

    The Controller — 54

    The Victim — 58

*How Attachment Styles Affect Relationships* — 62

    Struggling To Attach — 64

    Struggling With Insecurity — 65

    Remaining Emotionally Disorganized — 65

    Struggles with Trusting — 66

| | |
|---|---|
| Secure Love | 67 |
| Anxious Love | 68 |
| Dismissive Avoidant Love | 70 |
| Fearful Avoidant Love | 71 |
| Disorganized Love | 72 |

## **Changing Your Own Attachment Style** — **74**

| | |
|---|---|
| Unconscious Beliefs | 76 |
| The Connection Between Your Beliefs And Thoughts | 79 |
| The Cycle Of Thoughts, Feelings, And Behaviors | 81 |
| Overcoming Unconscious Beliefs | 85 |
| Rewriting Your Narrative and Changing Your Attachment Style | 88 |

## **Understanding Your Partner in Distress** — **93**

| | |
|---|---|
| Be Willing To Do It | 94 |
| Specialize In It | 96 |
| Be Calm | 98 |
| Give Them an Opportunity at their Blank Box | 101 |
| Read the Maps | 103 |
| Duck-Shove Complaints | 105 |

| | |
|---|---|
| Empathy | 107 |
| Set To Blend | 108 |
| Do It For Love | 110 |
| Don't Quit On Them: | 111 |
| Be Helpful | 113 |
| Ferrule their Flaws | 114 |
| Retain the Connection | 116 |
| Listen | 118 |
| Acknowledge Your Feelings | 119 |
| **Making Your Partner Understand You** | **121** |
| Don't Zero Your Mind | 122 |
| Talk | 124 |
| Exchange Love All The Time | 125 |
| Leave The Trails | 127 |
| Appreciate Them | 129 |
| Talk | 130 |
| Empathy | 134 |
| This Can't Get Overboard | 136 |
| Be Willing To Compromise | 138 |

| | |
|---|---|
| Give Your Partner A Chance | 140 |
| Invite Support | 141 |

## *Emotion-Focused Therapy (EFT) and Additional Practices*
## *143*

| | |
|---|---|
| Diving into Your Emotions | 145 |
| Identify What Feelings Were Present in the Conflict | 146 |
| Identify What Triggers Were Fired | 148 |
| Evaluate Your Level of Emotion | 150 |
| Expressing Your Emotions | 151 |
| Exploring Productive Ways to Respond: Diving Deeper | 161 |
| Reframing the Matter | 163 |
| Acceptance | 164 |

## *Conclusion*                                                        *169*

# Introduction

I want to thank and congratulate you for downloading this book, "***Attachment Style***."

History has a strange way of repeating itself. Over and over again, we discover that our relationships repeat in the same ways regardless of what we do.

We see ourselves repeating the mistakes in our relationships, changing how we interact with our partners, friends, children, and anyone else. This is often because we have common emotional reactions to people and relationships, beginning from childhood.

There is one single concept that will influence every relationship that you will ever have: Attachment.

We all have different attachment styles that affect what we do and the way we do them. Once we get attached to somebody else, we typically do so in several ways, and our attachment styles usually influence these.

We learn certain attachment styles based on our relationships with our parents, which become the most crucial in our lifetimes.

Research has shown that 60% of individuals have attachment styles that are secure and healthy—they have attachments, which will help them greatly to make sure that they will make the right kind of bonds to people around them. They have learned that they can trust relationships, that relationships are good, and will be approached and embraced.

However, that leaves 40% of individuals that don't have that healthy relationship pattern. 40% of individuals develop habits that aren't conducive to good, healthy relationships, instead of shifting toward either avoidant or anxious attachment styles.

What does this mean for people, you might be wondering? It means many of us wandering around in this world don't have healthy attachments. They do not have the inherent trust to make sure that their relationships are healthy, typically from some kind of trauma in childhood.

If you discover that you are in the 40% of individuals who have an unhealthy attachment style, then there is a good chance you are struggling to create relationships due to some trauma in the past that must be fixed.

In this book, you will discover the differences between these different attachment styles. You will learn what each looks like, taking the time to know secure, anxious, avoidant-dismissive, and avoidant-fearful attachment styles, seeing exactly how they have a tendency to influence people.

You will find out how you can tell your attachment style, allowing you to work out what your own current emotional attachment styles are.

Once you learn to know your approach to relationships, you will begin to work out what matters. You will begin to find out what you can do to help you influence your relationship with people. If you want to have healthy relationships in life, you will need to understand your own and your partner.

As you read through this book, you will discover ways to have a healthier relationship than ever before. You will learn to know how to deal with your partner's attachment style and the way you can develop your sense of self at the same time.

If you want to understand yourself and your relationships, you will discover what it will take you to ensure that you can let your past injuries heal, giving you the power that you will need.

Don't let your past define your future anymore. Find out how you can begin to learn more and find out what it will take so that you, too, can approach your relationships to facilitate and create trust and awareness. Whether you are trying to do better for your marriage or future relationships, this book will assist you.

Now, let's get started— let's dive right into taking a look at attachment styles and how we create them.

# Basics of Attachment Theory

Attachment theory is based on the underlying concept that attachment is the first mechanism in all our relationships, whether or not they are romantic, platonic, or familial. The attachment patterns that impact our everyday relationships are often transformed or exacerbated over time, counting on our life's circumstances. In order to find out ways to improve closeness and intimacy in relationships, these patterns must first be understood.

Our childhood experiences impact the traits that we express as adults. These impacts are revealed in what we will refer to as attachment styles. Although there is often an overlap between attachment styles, people do have the power to shift their attachment style over time. Let's imagine there is a lady named Chen. As a toddler, her parents were completely negligent. Due to drug abuse issues, neither parent was emotionally available or present in the moments Chen needed them the most. When Chen had challenges with schoolwork or problems being bullied at college, her parents did not notice. As a result, Chen came to believe that to survive; she had to be self-sufficient.

This belief became a part of her sense of self and was then brought into her friendships, romantic relationships, and perpetuation, even in her familial relationships.

Chen has struggled with being susceptible to others throughout her life due to her vulnerability as a toddler of negligent parents. Chen had friends and romantic partners but never felt deeply connected to them and couldn't understand why. She did not realize that her own belief patterns around attachment caused her to subconsciously avoid getting too close to others so as not to feel hurt again.

This is an example of only one attachment pattern that consistently occurs yet is never understood by the individuals themselves. It is essential for Chen to know how this happens so that she will transform what's creating loneliness and acting as a barrier to human connection.

This chapter will learn more about the origins of attachment theory and what attachment styles exist. Once you are equipped with these tools, you will have the inspiration to start transforming your relationships.

# What Is Attachment Theory?

Attachment theory is the study of how childhood experiences with our caregivers affect adulthood relationships. It had been jointly developed by John Bowlby and Mary Ainsworth in the 1960s. Mary Ainsworth was a graduate of the University of Toronto and specialized in security theory, which emphasizes a child's dependence on their caregiver. However, Ainsworth sought out an edge to work with Bowlby due to his reformulated approach to traditional psychology. Bowlby, a scholar from Cambridge University, was influenced by the professional relationship he had with two young boys upon graduating.

Bowlby became particularly curious about attachment when he began working with teenagers. One of the teenagers he worked with was a withdrawn, indifferent young man who lacked a mother figure. The other was a fearful child who was inseparable from Bowlby. According to The Origins of Attachment Theory, the second boy had parents who were either overbearing or entirely absent in his childhood. The stark difference between the two boys and their upbringing is what led Bowlby to start researching the correlation between upbringing and adult relationships. He wondered: Is there a connection between how a toddler is treated and how they then continue to treat others? This wonderment and his subsequent life's work try to answer the question he posed, which would be the inspiration for attachment theory.

Since the 1960s, attachment theory has gained significant traction and has been supported empirically by doctors and researchers alike. It has been carefully crafted into what it is today, which is a theory that clearly demonstrates how an individual's parenting affects their adult relationships.

## Types of Attachment Styles

Attachment styles, or the way in which different types of childhood experiences emerge in adulthood, are available in four basic forms:

— Dismissive-Avoidant
— Fearful-Avoidant
— Anxious Attachment
— Secure Attachment

### Dismissive-Avoidant

Someone with a Dismissive-Avoidant attachment style will:

— Generally, appear withdrawn
— Be highly independent
— Be emotionally distant in their relationships
— Be less likely to attach on an intimate level
— Find it difficult to be highly involved with their partners
— Become overwhelmed once they are relied on heavily
— Retreat physically and emotionally as a result

Their core beliefs, or the recurring perceptions that replay in their subconscious, will perpetuate a way of defectiveness and uncertainty in relationships. They essentially think at an innermost level that they are unsafe around people which vulnerability always leads to pain.

Although the Dismissive-Avoidant may appear to possess shortcomings in their relationships (as do those with all attachment styles), they will actually be wonderful partners. A relationship is often healthier, happier, and more fulfilling by having a deeper understanding of why someone is Dismissive-Avoidant.

So, why is the Dismissive-Avoidant individual so distant? Adults who are Dismissive-Avoidant typically had parents who were absent from their childhood. This absence is often in the kind of physical, emotional, or intellectual abandonment. Since children quite literally depend on their parents for survival, those with neglectful parents need to find out how to self-soothe. Eventually, this child is probably going to develop a belief that they can only safely believe themselves. This belief is then subconsciously brought into adulthood and manifests as distant and dismissive behavior. However, this will be remedied over time—a healthy relationship with a Dismissive-Avoidant is often built with consistent emotional support, autonomy, and direct communication.

**Fearful-Avoidant**

An individual who is Fearful-Avoidant will:

— Often demonstrate ongoing ambivalence in relationships—they continuously shift between being vulnerable with their partner and being distant. This behavior is consistent across all their relationships, no matter whether or not they are romantic.

— Generally express the depth of processing—a tendency to overanalyze micro-expressions, body language, and language for signs of betrayal. This happens because they had an untrusting relationship with their caregivers in childhood. Living with a parent who is an addict or emotionally unwell are two examples of what may create this distrust.

— Not trust naturally

— Often feel as if betrayal is usually on the horizon

The core wounds for this attachment style revolve around feeling unworthy, being taken advantage of, and feeling unsafe.

Why is the Fearful-Avoidant individual so unpredictable? Their core wounds and tumultuous behavior typically stem from some kind of childhood abuse. However, this abuse is paired with one or both parents also being emotionally supportive at infrequent times. This mix creates an innate sense of distrust and confusion, and Fearful-Avoidants learn to expect betrayal while also craving love. It also becomes quite difficult for the Fearful- Avoidant to find a technique for attaching or bonding to caregivers due to inconsistency.

Moreover, since they perceived love as a chaotic entity from a young age, they have a tendency to possess immense internal conflict as adults. They simultaneously want to feel a sense of connection while subconsciously believing it to be a threat. This produces feelings of resentment or frustration, which will be later projected onto relationships.

Ultimately, the Fearful-Avoidant shows up in their relationships as a loving partner; then, they will become frightened and shy away once they become vulnerable. To be in a successful relationship with a Fearful-Avoidant, the partner or friend must provide a deep connection in a consistent way. This means openness and respect for boundaries, paired with constant reassurance.

### Anxious Attachment

— Is generally highly self-sacrificing to "people-please"
— Fears rejection

— Has a robust fear of being abandoned?

Like the Fearful-Avoidant attachment style, the Anxious attachment style results from inconsistency in childhood. However, in the case of the Anxious Attachment, inconsistency is essentially derived from absenteeism instead of abuse by or the dysfunction of a caregiver.

Ultimately, what cultivates an Anxious Attachment in a child is the absence of a predictable and consistent caregiver. Their core wounds will include feelings of inadequacy, and the expectation of rejection since attention from their parent was continually given, then removed.

Inconsistent parenting also can be the result of a supportive but often absent parent or other scenarios where a parent has the capacity to attune to their child but not always the availability. Let's use the instance of Jonathan. Both of Jonathan's parents work in the military. They are both emotionally available and present with Jonathan throughout his childhood, but they work and travel a lot. One or both of his parents are often away for prolonged periods, and he's left to stay with his grandparents. This inconsistency leaves

Jonathan hungry for closeness to his parents. He understands what it means to be close and connected, as his parents have demonstrated this to him. However, the inconsistency becomes very painful for him, and he is always hungry for more closeness once they leave. The inconsistency leaves him hypervigilant and in fear of being abandoned. Since the subconscious learns patterns through whatever it is exposed to consistently, it eventually has a whole program around fearing abandonment.

Since one of the sole fears that we are biologically born with is the fear of abandonment, erratic parenting constantly triggers anxiety for the kid. This fosters a way of abandonment; then, they sacrifice their needs in adulthood to subconsciously maintain relationships.

The Anxious Attachment will often overcompensate in friendships and romantic relationships to avoid rejection, but this inevitably leads to resentment. For the Anxious Attachment, this is often because there is often confusion between compromise and sacrifice. They will often fail to acknowledge the difference between the two—one being a short-lived shift in needs versus the entire abandonment of them—and this often breeds conflict long-term. Over time, the Anxious Attachment can often perpetuate unhealthy habits, feel a scarcity of self-worth, and knowledge failed relationships.

Although the Anxious Attachment's core wounds trigger these feelings, they can be healed. Invalidating, available, and affectionate relationships, the Anxious Attachment are often a tremendous partner and truly grow into themselves.

**Secure Attachment**

Those with a Secure attachment style:

— Are secure in relationships
— Are generally supportive, available, and open with their friends or partners
— Can help shift those of other attachments into a safer space and, with the right tools, can ensure they become Secure also.

Secure Attachment arises from a childhood that has available and supportive parents. They were taught that you are often safe while being vulnerable that their needs were worth being met. In the early studies, children who were secure due to supportive parenting would freely explore when their caregiver was present but would become noticeably upset once they left.

Just as attachment styles are created, they will be transformed. The goal is to maneuver toward a Secure attachment style and far away from the aforementioned behaviors. Although other attachment styles don't indicate that somebody is inherently flawed, they will perpetuate unhealthy habits and reinforce negative beliefs.

By learning about the various attachment styles and the way they modify in several relationships, you will learn how to heal the dynamic between yourself, your partner, and the people closest to you.

You will be equipped to uncover your subconscious mechanisms and even reprogram your mind. Once you have got this information, you can truly begin to better yourself.

## Uses of Attachment Theory

According to the Association for Child and Adolescent psychological state (ACAMH), attachment theory is widely used by doctors, lawyers, politicians, and teachers alike. Since it helps explain the relationship between parenting and subsequent development, it is useful in a field where predicting and understanding behavior is important. Although it is especially helpful when understanding romantic relationships, it is often applied to friendships, familial relationships, and even behavior in the workplace.

Think about it—if you were to really understand why you behave the way you do, it could, for instance, help you get closure with your caregivers who were emotionally neglectful or incongruent in their parenting. Once you understand your internalized pain and how it affects you, you can be able to—with the techniques outlined later in this book—heal yourself and heal any relationships that your attachment style bleeds into.

For example, recall Parker from the previous section. As an adult, he fights with his partner daily because he feels as if he is always the one putting the trouble into the relationship. He moved into his partner's apartment in a different city, and he even switched his job to a new industry to do so. His resentment has grown, but he rationalizes his choices, saying that if he didn't do this stuff, the relationship "wouldn't work."

At work, he also feels concerned about his job security when his boss criticizes his projects. Although his boss just wants to move a project in a different direction, Parker takes it personally. With friends, he constantly feels concerned about giving them enough attention amid everything else happening. He is overwhelmed, resentful, and frustrated that he is not pursuing a career in something he is in love with.

Now, imagine Parker understood why he chose to do and to stress about these things. He has, at his core, an Anxious attachment style. He abandons his needs, as he perceives, to satisfy others to keep them in his life. However, actually, his growing resentment for his partner is poisoning his relationship. He is unfulfilled at work because he is in an industry he does not enjoy and is taking criticism personally no matter its intent. With friends, he cannot show up authentically due to everything else that he has on his plate—which causes him immense distress due to the programs running in his subconscious.

In each of those cases, Parker needs only to understand that a healthier version of his life lies in understanding why he makes these choices and their true consequences. By understanding his attachment style, he will be able to compromise instead of sacrifice in his relationship, understand the importance of authentically following his career aspirations, and remove some anxiety from his friendships by understanding that a friend won't just disappear.

Although all this alteration is easier said than done, this surface-level example sheds some light on how understanding your attachment style truly impacts every area of your life.

Now that you better understand the widespread application of attachment theory, we will also explore the ways in which it also functions across professions like the medical field, legal field, children's education, and public policy. Not only can attachment theory be applied to different relationships, but it is also often used to understand the functionality of various macro-level scenarios better. For instance, in children's education, understanding attachment theory enables teachers and caretakers to understand better students' interactions, another example described by the ACAMH. If one student is exhibiting withdrawn behavior, it will be important for the teacher to offer the student the space they need to process their emotions before approaching them to discuss the matter. Moreover, applying attachment theory can also indicate whether there is aggressive or violent behavior occurring in an adolescent's home, according to research.

Furthermore, if the student is continually demonstrating ambivalent behavior, like aggressive conflict resolution, it will indicate a volatile household. By properly identifying the difficulty, the teenager might be removed and delivered to safety. Similar applications of attachment theory are often seen across all professions. Ultimately, attachment theory helps one understand the ways in which people function on a personal level and while interacting with each other.

Although attachment theory has many applications, it tends to be especially useful in couples' therapy. Since each attachment style has generalized trends, understanding your or your partner's coping mechanisms, subconscious beliefs, and perceptions can relieve substantial communication issues. For instance, in a relationship, the Dismissive-Avoidant could also be withdrawn, autonomous, and seemingly independent. To the Dismissive-Avoidant, they are functioning as they always have—on their own. To an Anxious Attachment, however, it will feel as if their partner is on the verge of abandoning them and should cause serious emotional distress. However, the Dismissive-Avoidant's coping mechanisms don't necessarily mean they are detaching from the relationship—they are literally just detaching from their own emotions.

Now, although none of those behaviors are necessarily healthy in a relationship, understanding why they occur is the initiative. Once partners understand each other's coping mechanisms and vulnerabilities, they will begin to provide their partners with the things that they need. For instance, Dismissive-Avoidant needs continuous and unwavering emotional support and validation. Since they were emotionally neglected as a toddler, they have to learn that they can consistently and predictably believe others slowly.

The Anxious Attachment individual needs reassurance and affection to know that they are okay and won't be rejected. The simple knowledge of your partner's pain points and the pain points that lie in yourself exposes an entire stream of communication that you previously were unable to tap into—because your conscious mind did not even realize it was there.

Moreover, your attachment style also interacts with what Dr. Gary Chapman describes as your "Love Language." Even if there are different spoken languages and different dialects present in the spoken languages, Love Languages are alternative ways people express and receive love or gratitude when interacting with others, whether with a romantic partner or with friends and family. According to Dr. Chapman's book, they contain five different types of expressions:

— Words of affirmation
— Acts of service
— Giving and receiving gifts
— Quality time
— Physical touch

Given the attachment type of each partner in a relationship, certain expressions could also be better received. Attachment theory applies to a spread of circumstances and works well paired with other theories to make couples therapy a more holistic experience. The subsequent chapters will dive into what your attachment style is, what it means, and the way it functions in all aspects of your life—from your romantic relationships to your friendships with coworkers.

## Finding Your Attachment Style

As the subconscious processes more information, core beliefs are often rewritten, and attachments will consequently shift.

Traditionally, attachment styles are viewed and applied to individuals as static characterizations. In other words, when someone knows they are Dismissive-Avoidant, they often believe they are solely that attachment style. However, this is often a surface-level explanation. It acknowledges their first attachment style, but people are literally composed of every attachment type in several proportions. Suppose a toddler had parents who were both abusive and emotionally negligent. In that case, they will express a stronger combination of Dismissive-Avoidant and Fearful-Avoidant characteristics, with the latter likely being more dominant. They might then have a lower proportion of Secure Attachment and Anxious

Attachment tendencies. This is often because attachment styles exist along a spectrum.

This is why an individual's attachment style can flex in several relationships—someone might be on the more anxious side of Fearful-Avoidant, for instance, counting on the number and significance of the experiences they have had. Supporting this claim, a recent study released from the University of Ottawa examined the relationships of 2,214 individuals.

It revealed that somebody might have a substantially different attachment with their parents, for instance, then they do with a partner with a Secure attachment style. Again, this reinforces the thought of attachment styles existing along a sliding spectrum. As individuals encounter new events and relationships that reinforce or disprove their subconscious beliefs, their attachment can shift over time.

This brings up the most important question for healing your attachment style: what is an attachment trauma?

Begin by recalling that your attachment style is actually a group of beliefs about human interaction that is ingrained in your subconscious. Since your subconscious is programmed through a mixture of repetition and emotion, your attachment style is made through repetitive events that induce strong feelings like fear or loneliness.

Your subconscious essentially involves believing what it perceives it is told over time.

To illustrate this idea, imagine there is a woman named Sophie. She experienced physical abuse as a toddler and has come to feel unsafe and uncomfortable while being vulnerable in her romantic relationships. However, Sophie's partner, Riley, has a Secure Attachment because supportive parents raised her. Consequently, Riley continuously supports Sophie and validates her emotions. This makes Sophie feel deserving of love and safe in the relationship. Over time, Sophie's subconscious belief that vulnerability is unsafe begins to be reprogrammed because Riley has shown her through a mixture of repetition plus emotion that her childhood subconscious beliefs are outdated. This is often how one begins to shift into a special type of attachment in a specific relationship. However, Sophie could still be subject to abuse when she sees her parents, which is what perpetuates her Fearful-Avoidant side in her parental relationship.

This occurrence is often seen across all attachment styles and may even be reversed for the secure partner. Imagine that Riley has a good relationship with Sophie, but that she also has a close friend who begins to treat Riley poorly. The friend constantly overwhelms Riley with information about her life but does not take the time to concentrate on what is happening in Riley's life. The friend even goes thus far on criticize Riley when Riley attempts to open up to her. Slowly, Riley's subconscious begins to think that she is undeserving of receiving the love that she gives. Then, in all of her friendships, she begins to develop a Fearful-Avoidant attachment. She becomes uncomfortable with vulnerability and begins to self-sacrifice more frequently. Without recognizing these subconscious patterns, Riley will still put herself through emotional turmoil and can begin to self-sacrifice to please friends as her subconscious beliefs get perpetuated.

To better understand how attachment style in one relationship type can continue to affect other relationships of the same type negatively, the

University of Kansas conducted a study that evaluated two aspects of platonic attachment styles:

— Tie strength: how close the ties are in an individual's network.
— Multiplexity: what percentage roles are filled by individuals in the network.

This study noted that those that had high Avoidant tendencies had weaker tie strength and multiplexity. However, those that were Anxious were significantly less likely to dissolve the ties, but friends would often feel smothered and make moves to dissolve the connection themselves.

The University of Kansas study demonstrates the latter of a two-part proposition:

— That attachment styles can change supported type—for example, friendship or a romantic relationship.
— That how an individual behaves in one relationship—for example, with one specific friend—can spread to how they behave in other relationships of that very same type- like with other friends. This idea is vital because it truly demonstrates the power of the subconscious to

store and replay beliefs based on repetition and emotion.

Now that you understand the fluidity of attachment styles and why they lie along a spectrum, you can begin to get your dominant attachment style in several areas of your life. Consider how you act and feel in your relationships, whether or not they are romantic, platonic, or familial. Examine the ratio of activating to deactivating strategies in your thoughts and behaviors. Recall that activating strategies are decisions that are made based on prior information and experiences. Deactivating strategies are actions that drive self-reliance and deny attachment needs altogether, pushing others away. If you have relatively more activating strategies, you may have a greater fear of abandonment and get on the Anxious side of the spectrum. More deactivating strategies may indicate a subconscious belief around complete autonomy, placing you more on the Dismissive-Avoidant side of the attachment scale.

Keep in mind that this tool should be used in romantic relationships after the honeymoon phase is over, a phase that happens in the first two years of the connection. According to Scientific American, in the honeymoon phase, your brain has higher levels of dopamine in the caudate and ventral tegmental regions. These areas of the brain are responsible for, respectively, learning and memory and emotional processing. Consequently, your attachment style could also be unclear to you in the early phases of your romantic relationship since your emotions, memory, and hormone regulation are atypical.

Our experiences also can dramatically alter our attachment style. For instance, if Sophie were to partake in certain types of therapy and practices like recurrent meditation, she could also be able to understand better and re-equilibrate her subconscious beliefs. According to Science Daily, since meditation induces theta brain waves and activates areas of the lobe related to emotional regulation, Sophie could eventually bring herself into a safer attachment space without the assistance of a Secure partner.

However, although it is common to precise different attachment styles in several areas of life, the type of attachment you have in relationships ultimately tends to be the attachment style you associate with the type of relationship. For instance, you can be Dismissive-Avoidant in familial relationships because you experienced emotional neglect from parental figures, but you can also be Fearful-Avoidant in romantic relationships due to domestic abuse that has occurred. This illustrates that major events like betrayal, loss, or abuse can alter our attachment style in several chapters of life, but that ultimately attachment styles are fluid and sometimes hooked into the type of relationships we are in.

We tend to have a first attachment style, most related to how we show up in romantic relationships, that plays a big role in our personality structure. This essentially dictates how we give and receive love and what our subconscious expectations are of others.

Now that you have the background on what attachment styles are, how they are formed, and in what ways they will be shaped and shifted, take the test below. Here you will learn your primary attachment style and—eventually—how you can move toward a Secure type of attachment.

# Dealing with Different Personalities

Now, we are beginning to get a little deeper. You have checked out the various attachment styles, and now it is time to look at love styles. We all love people differently. We all show ourselves in our relationships differently, as well. Typically, these are relationship styles developed over time and are highly influenced by those attachment styles. They will create different types of interactions for you and the people around you.

Typically, people in relationships usually have one of five approaches to how they plan to address the relationship as a whole. They will address their partners differently depending on what they have learned in life. Typically, like attachment style, the love styles also are highly influenced by those old patterns. The relationships that were developed with the parents once more come into play here, altering how you want to look at how you engage with your partners.

As you read through this chapter, you will meet the five commonest approaches to relationships that people take. Typically, you will find that people are either avoidant, pleasers, controllers, or victims in relationships. They will find there is some kind of middle ground, but usually, you will identify one over the other in somebody else. The earlier you begin to know your partner's type of person, the sooner you start to see how your partner will interact in your relationships, the earlier that you can start to work out the way to interact. If you recognize that your partner falls into the avoider type, you can then extrapolate from that understanding and infer that they are likely to keep to themselves, which is not a slight at you. If they have a tendency to always say yes to you, they could be a pleaser and just want to make sure that they don't rock the boat.

As you read through this chapter, try to think about what kind of person you are. Check out the traits that you will see here. Concentrate on the behaviors, then start to spot whether you think you fall under one of these patterns of behaviors. Additionally, think about your partner, as well. Where do they have a tendency to fall under this? Are they avoidant? Do they bend over backward for you? Do they struggle to gain control of everything? There is probably a reason for it—and understanding who your partner is as an individual will help you greatly with trying to work out the way to expect the relationship to play out.

## The Pleaser

Do you find that everything you are doing, you are doing because you would like to keep the peace? Is the word "No," not in your vocabulary? Will you do almost anything for anyone to figure out what it will take to keep everyone around you happy?

If that sounds familiar, you are potentially a pleaser. Typically, pleasers are the kind of people that have grown up in a home that is either too protective or has a critical parent. Effectively, the parent is just too reactive in some way or the other, and the child has learned that he or she has to try to keep the peace to avoid problems afterward. It is easier only to give the parent what they want instead of trying to say anything. As an immediate result, the pleaser tends to fall under the trap of making sure that everybody else around them is happy.

The pleaser thinks that they are unimportant in life; their presence is optional or is merely really there to make sure that everybody else is happy. They don't believe they are deserving of comfort, and they certainly don't ask for anything either. They understand that everybody around them is more likely to get what they need than anything else, which is a sacrifice that they are willing to make.

Typically, the name of the game for the pleaser is to make as few waves as possible—they do what they will be the great child, the one that doesn't need anything ever that their parents aren't worried about them constantly. Instead of being the source of strife, they feel like it is their job to support their parents.

In adulthood, pleasers typically then extrapolate that to mean that they can't have what they need. They grind to a halt into the thought that ultimately, they are there to support people. They are there to make sure that the people in their lives are happy. They are the peacekeepers in the relationships, and they will sacrifice their happiness if they need to, even though they will secretly resent it constantly. They think that it is expected, and thus, they will make a sacrifice without a complaint.

If you are wondering if you are a pleaser or if your partner is one, try considering these points:

People always describe me as the good one—the one that never caused any problems and was quiet and just fine left to my very own devices.

Having someone upset at me is distressing, and that I would rather make my sacrifices than deal with people being upset or directing negative emotions my way.

I want connection and seek it out, and I avoid rejection by ensuring that I can always meet the requirements of those around me, even if it is difficult for me or if I don't want to do what I'm doing.

Conflict is difficult to deal with, so I might rather just concede to avoid the entire situation; I'll admit fault even if it is disingenuous because I'd rather avoid the fight.

Saying no is difficult, even when it is something that I should be just fine saying no about. Even though it is a matter of opinion, I can't say no—I would rather nod my head and say I like something that I hate than be placed on the spot or potentially upset somebody else.

Is your partner a people pleaser? If so, it is probably frustrating for you, especially because you would like to offer and receive the healthiest relationships. You have to make sure that your partner is cared for and can't tell if they are or not once they aren't willing to be forthright with their feelings. Once you are in a relationship with a pleaser, you will regularly be worrying if your partner is happy in the first place. To try to cope, try considering the following points:

— **Set boundaries**: If your partner is not the one to set the boundaries, you can do so. Because they need to repeatedly please you don't mean that you need to do the same—set boundaries and let your partner see-through modeling that it is okay to say no sometimes. It is okay to prioritize self-care sometimes, and the sooner that you teach your partner this, the better.

— **Control your anger**: It is often frustrating to see your partner constantly being taken advantage of—but remember, he or she is an adult. You can't change your partner. All you can do is control your reaction to things. Avoid pushing his or her emotions and allow them to work on their feelings themselves.

— **Be neutral**: Let your partner know that you are there—but be unbiased about it. Don't try to fix your partner's problems and easily allow them to know that you are present and happy to listen.

— **Encourage choices**: Ask your partner to settle on dinner or what you will do this night. Make sure that they know they have a say too, and encourage them to make those choices. Allow them to choose hobbies or movies sometimes. Make yourself a secure place for your partner to practice making choices.

## The Avoider

Do you find that you like people but struggle with their emotions? Maybe you like the idea of people—but you don't want to try to work out people's emotions. Do you prefer not to rely on anyone, and likewise, feel annoyed when people rely on you? If so, you may be an avoider.

Avoiders are people that often were denied the love that they craved as a toddler. They are people that found that affection, or wanting affection, was nothing but a weakness that might end in disappointment, even though, really, they wanted it more than anything. They learned that ultimately, also trying to get that affection isn't well worth the effort, and somewhere along the way, they gave up trying.

For the avoider, the most crucial part of who they are is typically their independence. The avoiders in the world pride themselves on not needing anyone, thinking that basically, it makes them strong. They don't see a reason they ought to be trying to get more out of a relationship. They see reliance on somebody else as a weakness, and because of that, they seek to avoid it at all costs. They need to be near people, but they also want to deal with themselves and their problems without counting on others.

However, as a result, they typically just push people away. They cut themselves off emotionally, and as an immediate result, they find that they can't get the support that we as people need. Rather than being willing to see the reality, they have to be ready to address and identify how they will engage with others; they find it far easier to cut them off easily. They will wall off their hearts, and they will fight tooth and nail to get on their own.

Of course, they also want to be somewhat close to people also for the social aspect—but only the fun parts. They want to coexist with someone else rather than find that they are a valuable source of support. It is better to exist near one another easily instead of making any real effort in getting along as far as they are concerned, and as an immediate result, they almost come off as abrasive.

Do you think that you could be an avoider? Is your partner an avoider? Consider these points—if they sound familiar, it may be the case that you are:

I typically can get past bad situations quickly—when something goes wrong, I will be able to shrug it off and keep moving forward. There is no real value in getting upset about it anyway—that is weakness generally.

It is better only to move forward and advance without fear about it.

Growing up, I found that talking about personal business or feelings was banned, and as an adult, I'm happy to continue living my life that way. The world isn't built upon feelings— it is built upon actions, and I intend to act instead of feel as much as possible.

Typically, I'm more comfortable once I realize that others around me are perfectly happy and that my presence isn't required for them to feel happy. I would like to make sure that I can disappear without ruining the lives of those around me—they are happier, not counting on me anyway.

I don't address or think about my emotional feelings or thoughts very often—I push them aside. I don't have to worry about them anyway—I will be just fine, regardless of what happens.

When I'm far away from my family or my partners, I don't mind much—I don't think about missing them. I kind of just like the space that I can get to do whatever it is that I wanted at the instant. Who wants to be needy anyway?

Is your partner an avoider? Having an avoidant partner is often frustrating if you would like to understand what is happening in their mind. While an avoider can seem perfect initially, you recognize that basically, they are going to be silent about their wants and wishes. Do they love you, or are they only keeping the peace? Are they only trying to run far away from their problems by agreeing? Do they like you when they seem to be so stoic? If your partner is avoidant, try considering the following actions:

Try to relate to them: this is often perhaps one of the best answers—try to work out how you can relate to them so that you can start to really understand. Try empathizing with them, hear what you think is their problems. Try to see where they are coming from. This will help make things a little more tolerable. Encourage emotional connection: make sure that you regularly ask your partner and remember that they are probably with you for a reason. At the very least, avoidant individuals will leave if they are uninterested. There is probably a reason that they are there, even though they keep their distance.

## The Vacillator

Do you want those relationships with people around you so badly that you would do almost anything for them? Do you end up more hesitant to want them once you realize that people will let you down anyway? Do you want to find out how to attach, but as long as it does not hurt you somehow? If so, you would possibly be a vacillator.

These people are those that grew up with unpredictable parents. While children, their needs didn't matter—they weren't the top priority for their parents, and as a result, they struggled to get the love they craved regularly. They felt like they could not really get any of the attention that every child loves and craves. Their parents may have been careless, too busy, or genuinely unaware of things. However, regardless of the reason, the child found that they struggled with feelings of abandonment.

Those feelings of abandonment become a defining feature for the vacillator's life—they assume that they will be continuously abandoned. The vacillator may constantly be chasing after breadcrumbs of attention from his or her parents. Still, as soon as their parent becomes curious about giving again, the child has given up. The child has found that they have waited too long and do not care to receive the results. They are too frustrated, too angry, and merely unreceptive, even though they now have access to what they wanted in the first place. As an immediate result, they find themselves feeling like they mattered even less because their parents didn't give until they were so furious in the first place.

In adulthood, however, vacillators are continually seeking to overcompensate. They have to make up for what they lost. They have to figure out what they will do to fi the hole that has developed for them, but unfortunately, nothing can fill that hole. They are constantly looking out for consistent, stable love in their lives. They are desperate for it. They are going to spend all kinds of time finding a relationship, then diving into it head-first, idealizing it, and treating it like what they have been missing all along.

Unfortunately, however, there is a problem; there is no single relationship in this world that is perfect. There is not one relationship that will not have conflict at some point. If you would like a real relationship with somebody else, there will be conflicts sometimes. This is often only natural—and to the vacillator, it is unacceptable. The vacillator wants perfection that does not exist and, as an immediate result, finds that his or her efforts are pointless. There is no reason they ought to try to achieve an impossible ideal continuously. It only serves to set them off more and make them more and more frustrated or jaded.

If you wonder if you are a vacillator in life, try considering these points. If they ring true, there is an opportunity that you do fit this pattern for your relationships:

No matter the situation, I have always felt like nobody ever really understands me or what it is that I want out of my relationships. They don't seem to get that I want consistency, which stresses me out. When I'm in a relationship, I find that I suffer from many internal conflicts—I ask myself what I'm doing and if it is worthwhile to be in this relationship constantly. I'm always questioning everything, and it causes high levels of emotional stress for me in my relationships.

Sometimes, I find that I'm making an argument and that I can't find out why. I'm picking a fight with my partner, almost as if to check them to see their reactions. Once I get that fight that I asked for, *I exploit it as justification that the connection was broken in the first place.*

I'm sensitive, and I know when the other party is pulling away from me. I can tell when they are getting ready to break up with me, and I am often prepared for it before it hits. I would like to be able to protect myself from making sure that I don't get hurt more. I'd even break it off before they will because it is easier than handling the pain.

I've heard, maybe more than once, that people in my life feel like they are always walking on eggshells when I'm around. They act as if they need to tiptoe around my feelings for a few reasons, and that I don't understand why.

If you are in a relationship with a vacillator, you almost certainly feel like you are on a rollercoaster, and for a good reason. They are always up and down and all over the place. However, you can support them. You can help them move past their childhood anger and help them become healthier, someone who can deal with their problems head-on. Of course, it takes time, effort, and possibly counseling. If your partner is a vacillator, consider the following:

Acknowledge that the vacillator is angry: you can start by helping your partner recognize that they are angry. That anger probably came from long before you ever entered the scene. You can see that your partner had idealized the future in hopes of trying to deal with their lives at the instant when things were terrible.

Of course, this ended up in all kinds of unrealistic expectations.

Remind your partner that it is okay not to be perfect: Pain is a part of all relationships. It is okay for there to be miscommunications sometimes, and encourage your partner to inform you about theirs once they arise. Let your partner know that you want to know when there is a problem and fix it together. Ask what your partner needs: make sure that your partner knows that you want to offer them what they need. Make sure that they feel supported that you can help them as much as you can.

## The Controller

Do you find that you want to always be on top of things and comfortable? Do you continuously try to take hold of situations because it is easier to be responsible than to be taken advantage of? These are telltale signs that you could also be a controller in your relationship.

Controllers are ultimately seeking protection—they don't want to be controlled or influenced by people. They don't want to be vulnerable, so they do everything that they can to be in charge. They will make it a point to keep all of their negativity inside and try to hide from those feelings because they are too painful to deal with. They think that the childhood struggles they have faced mean that they need to learn a valuable lesson—they need to protect themselves at all costs. They have learned that protection comes from a sense of control, and likewise, they are going to make use of anger as a way of protecting themselves. Anger is the one that they feel isn't vulnerable so that they use it to maintain that control even longer.

Typically, controllers are quite rigid in their relationships—they struggle to be willing to deal with their feelings in ways in which they feel are inefficient. They need control in everything, and they will do whatever it takes to maintain it.

If you think that you could also be a controller, consider these points:

> — I feel like nobody ever protected me when I was younger, and as a result, I learned from the varsity of adversity. I'm who I am today because I had to learn to take care of myself instead of wait for somebody else to guard me.

— I believe only two types of people in this world are controlled or those in control. I would like to be the person in control.
— I'm regularly described as intimidating or angry, even though I'm pretty sure I'm just firm.
— I typically try to solve my problems because people around me aren't reliable anyway. I will be able to take care of things on my own instead of making myself vulnerable.
— I want things to be done my way or the highway, and if it is not my way, I will be angry about it. After all, I will at least do it correctly.

If you are currently in a relationship with a controller, there is a good chance that you are part of the problem. It is highly likely that you are codependent—controllers aren't healthy partners. They need everything their way, which is inherently problematic in a relationship. If you discover that you are in a relationship with a controller, you have to find out a way to fix the relationship somehow. You will need to take on some accountability yourself here and try doing the following:

— Recognize that you are in control: While your partner could also be controlling you, recognize that basically, the only control they have is that you are allowing them to. Nobody has any control over you without your consent, and you can remove that consent whenever you choose to.
— Find new people to hang out with: Sometimes, removing yourself from a situation is enough to make it better. See if you can surround yourself with healthier individuals.
— Recognize that you can say no: Teach yourself to say no when it matters. There is no reason that you have to concede because your partner demanded it. You can soothe yourself and teach yourself that you can make your own decisions on your own.

## The Victim

Do you find that it is easier to only keep quiet and ignore your own needs? Do you know your needs, or do you find that you couldn't identify them even if you tried? If you are feeling like it is easier to let things happen without ever trying to take care of yourself, you would possibly be the victim type.

Typically, people that play the victim role are known for being compliant. They stayed under the radar and learned that it is better to be invisible than to be the target of anger or chaos. They even have these vast, big words that they create for themselves that they use as shields to guard themselves against those around them. They typically are lacking in any meaningful self-worth and typically are too anxious or depressed to enjoy life.

In adulthood and their relationships, they often find that they are happier marrying a controller than using compliance to avoid getting through life. It is easier just to be controlled by the victim, and they would rather do this than anything.

If you think that you could be a victim, consider the following points:

— I typically was angry or stressed by my parents or might take out their stress and anger on me. I learned it is just easier to close up and avoid the matter altogether.

- I don't mind living in chaos—at least things can't worsen when things are already chaotic. When things are calm, you have to stress about problems arising.
- Speaking up is merely going to cause more problems at the end of the day, so I'd rather just close up and deal with the issues face.
- I usually feel like I'm just going through the motions because it is easier than trying to change anything.

If your partner is the victim type, what do you do? It is often challenging to listen to someone who insists that it is not their fault that they are suffering. However, there are ways in which you can deal with this personality type to make sure that your partner comes out of it. Remember, this is often a result of childhood, more often than not, and it will take time. Keep in mind that the mindset often remains attractive for the victim—it is simpler to play the victim who has no blame in a situation than it is to admit that you could also be wrong, after all.

To deal with this type of person in a relationship, consider the following:

— Empathize and listen, but disagree: it is essential to support your partner, and you can do this through listening and acknowledging those feelings but don't justify them.
— Don't make them feel like they are right for what they feel. Disagree—that will just reinforce the pattern. Point out the flaws: While empathizing with the victim mentality partner, make sure that you are also willing to point out that they are stuck. Let them know that they will actually do something—point out or gently guide your partner toward some solutions and encourage them to pursue them.
— Encourage responsibility: the only possible way to break free from this mindset is to learn to accept accountability, which is difficult frequently. Let your partner see that there are better ways to get through life—they can accept that they have a problem, but it is not the end of the world. The earlier that you acknowledge this, the better.
— Teach them to respect themselves: Finally, make sure that you teach your partner that they matter. Allow them to know that they owe it to

themselves to help themselves and make themselves healthier and better. It will help.

# How Attachment Styles Affect Relationships

Every human is programmed to bond with their mothers. Most mammals are. Have you ever seen the bond between the human newborn and mother? The newborn is preprogrammed to be in tune with her voice, her heart, and her smell.

A newborn is programmed to crawl up to the breast to nurse. The act of nursing comes instinctively to release those self-same bonding hormones that release in sex and orgasm. The entire purpose of the hormones and people's earliest interactions is to bond one infant to at least one mother.

Yes, lately, we have substitutes for breast milk, but in nature and before civilization, infants that did not have their mothers present for milk wouldn't easily survive. Milk was essential to the newborn's survival; that bond between infant and mother, then, was developed to be immensely powerful. You look to your mother for her responsiveness. You look to your mother for her to interact with you. You would like her to show you and to appease you. Your first emotional attachment was to your first primary caregiver, and for the overwhelming majority of humanity, that is the mother.

Your entire species is made upon this; it might not survive without that connection. Think about it—the average human child will nurse readily and frequently for years if left to their own devices. Biologically speaking, human offspring will breastfeed for up to 7 years in some cases, not too far away from the lengths of your time of a number of our closest relatives. Orangutan mothers breastfeed until around age 8 or 9.

Chimpanzee mothers breastfeed to age 5 and gorillas until age 4. This shows that even in closely related species, you have that constant first connection for years—the infants or children rely on their mothers for survival. While we have adapted and developed other solutions, like providing cow's milk in toddlerhood and infancy to substitute out that milk, those bonds still matter. We are genetically predisposed to possess those desires for attachment just to survive, so what happens when those attachments are broken or damaged?

Attachment shapes the brain; it changes how we interact with people, and it can directly influence how you relate to your partner in adulthood. It directly affects how we will interact with other adults, and insecurity can become a lifelong problem if you don't manage to find out how to deal with it. If you are not careful, you will create a situation where you can't properly deal with or bond with those around you.

Insecure attachment in adulthood can directly influence the relationships that you will build. If you would like to get married and have children, you have to be ready to have healthy attachments in the first place. That will be difficult to make it happen; however, you can't properly do so if you don't know what you are doing. Let's take a number of the most common ways in which insecure attachment will show up in those adult relationships so you can start to know what you can do to fix the issues.

## Struggling To Attach

When you never get to connect with your parents, it becomes incredibly difficult to open up to anyone. The connection with your parents needs to be the most secure one that you have, and when that one fails, the rest will also. Failure typically happens due to having parents that are either unavailable, physically or mentally, or having self-absorbed parents. As a result, children tend to work on themselves, turning inward, while adults prefer to remain distant in every relationship they need.

## Struggling With Insecurity

When you find that you have inconsistent or intrusive parents, you may also find that you struggle to understand what comes next. Because you struggle with insecurity, you discover that you never know what to expect and, therefore, never respond accordingly. When it comes right down to the relationships you have in adulthood, you may be available one moment before completely shutting down for your partner the next, leaving them feeling like they are affected by whiplash.

## Remaining Emotionally Disorganized

Emotional disorganization comes from feeling like you can't bond with anyone that you meet. You discover that ultimately, the interactions that you have are difficult to navigate. You struggle to like, and you may become unable to know the emotions of those around you. You will find that you can't read your partner at all, and as an immediate result, you run into all kinds of other problems.

When you struggle with having the ability to express yourself in childhood, you will probably never develop the talents that you need to make yourself more effective at doing so. You will never learn how you can find out the way to manage your emotions, and because of that, you struggle in adulthood with your anger and aggression. You might even implement it toward your partner because you always received the anger as a toddler from your parents. You learn that you have to redirect the anger toward the person you are supposed to be close to in relationships.

## Struggles with Trusting

You might find that trust is difficult to come by. You are slow to trust if you ever do it in the first place. You will find that you are unwilling to make it a point to interact with those in your life because you feel like the pain isn't worthwhile.

# Secure Love

In terms of being in a relationship, those that learned to like securely because of having secure bonds with their parents are usually quite comfortable in romantic relationships. They feel just fine being alone or being in a relationship, though they typically like better to have those relationships for companionship. They have to be in relationships not because they need to, but because they enjoy feeling both needed and trusted by somebody else.

Securely attached people tend to find out a way for them to work out how they will maintain their independence in their life while still managing to do it with their partners. They may be jealous sometimes, but they are capable of handling these feelings and problems for the most part. They are usually quite relaxed and trusting. They are willing to make those connections with their partners, and they are the healthiest in relationships. They are more satisfied with their relationships, and they feel like their romantic partner is a directly reliable source of support. They feel secure and connected to their partners at all times, meaning that navigating the world is better than ever, and they can work on themselves while knowing that their partners are there for them.

In their relationship, securely attached couples usually offer that support needed when one person is feeling distressed or unable to move forward. They will comfort one another and make sure that they are all able to feel better about themselves. They are the go-to source of comfort for their partners without feeling like they are too needy. They will be honest and equal with one another, without acting like they are on one another's nerves for needing each other.

## Anxious Love

Relationships marked by the anxious preoccupied types are typically getting to struggle. They typically create what we call a fantasy bond— they need to be wanted or loved so that they set themselves up for what they think they have, even if that is not a real relationship or real bond. They do not truly feel love or trust—they feel a pang of emotional hunger. They feel a desire for his or her partner, to complete them. They are trying to find a rescuer, for somebody to make them feel like they matter and trust one another. This is often imperative; they have it to make themselves feel like they will get to that point with one another. They seek a way of safety and feel secure in a relationship, but without actually making it a point to relate. They push their partners away without really bothering to relate well to them.

The people that fall for this category are directly acting in ways in which will make things worse. Remember to the knowledge provided earlier in which the idea that you have will directly influence feelings and behaviors. This happens here—the anxiety usually makes the behaviors that create worse tension in the future. Once they feel like their partners are pulling away, they tend to react by becoming possessive or clingy, which only pushes their partners away. They will find that they are regularly pushing their partners to find out what it will take them to be loved, only to understand that the more they push, the larger the rift they are creating. They will be terrified and clingy, and when their partner starts hanging out with people or tries to make it a point to take care of independence and autonomy, they decide that their partner does not love them after all.

# Dismissive Avoidant Love

In dismissive-avoidant relationships, you will find that the dismissive individual typically will seek emotional distance at all times. They seek to force that they are independent, effectively isolating themselves, and focus on themselves. While independence is vital in any relationship, it is also a big problem if you can't develop it appropriately. Independence matters, but independence to the point of never focusing on a partner are merely two people claiming that they are in a relationship without ever engaging. Consider the stereotypical two ships passing out stumped —you are never actually connecting. All relationships form upon connection, yet those with dismissive avoidant attachment styles will typically avoid it. They specialize in themselves inwardly.

Typically, you will expect to find out this person feeling like they don't care to interact or connect with their partner. They would really like to be emotionally packed up and sometimes described as having boundaries around themselves. They may, in heated moments, respond by turning off their emotions entirely. They don't react at all. If their partner is stressed, they respond by not caring anymore. They tell their partner that they are not actually interested or maybe invested in what is happening—they completely disengage entirely without much interest in trying to fix things.

## Fearful Avoidant Love

When it involves fearful-avoidant relationships, new problems form, the fearful-avoidant individual lives in a state of ambivalence—they don't want to be too close or too distant at the same time, creating a kind of paradox. They need to be close to their partners in life, but at the same time, they worry that if they get too close to their partners, they will be hurt. They plan to feel distant, and they try to feel like they are not attached, but when that inevitable attachment occurs, they find that they are unable to avoid their anxiety.

They become overwhelmed with the emotions and typically become emotionally turbulent—they are oscillating between moods to the point of unpredictability. They need to get close, and they know that if you want your needs met, you have to be close to people, but that very same closeness creates an emotional vulnerability. They fear that vulnerability—they don't want to be in a position in which they will get hurt, and because they are, they find that they are terrified. Effectively, they need to go toward their partner for safety, but at the same time, they are terrified to get close. They are scared of the repercussions. They worry that if they struggle to get closer, they are going to struggle.

This is perhaps one of the most complicated relationship patterns that you can see—the attachment style renders the individual in a position in which the relationship is rocky. There are highs and lows to be experienced, and as they occur, there are many situations in which the individual may feel trapped, rejected, and miserable, all at the same time. The fearful-avoidant attachment type is especially susceptible to abusive relationships.

## Disorganized Love

You may find that disorganized love is usually left off of lists, but it is also the most extreme insecure attachment types. In a relationship, this type of attachment style, the child learns that life isn't safe—they know that even people that they recognize or are supposed to trust are often feared, and as a result, they struggle. They feel anxiety and fear in their relationships but also want to be loved. They have a real desire for their relationships to work, and they want to attach to people, but the constant stress and wondering if their partner is going to hurt them is enough to cause erratic behavior.

Of course, those erratic behaviors also directly influence the relationship. The more erratic the behaviors, the more likely it is that the relationship will generally fail. This has nothing to do with the individual involved at all, and it is everything to do with how the one with a disorganized attachment style has learned to work. This particular type of relationship forms through trauma and distress. It stems from being unable to work out how they ought to answer any given setup. They frequently struggle with how they will learn what matters. They can't learn what their bond should look like, and they find themselves oscillating between the extremes so much that they never know what they need to be doing.

# Changing Your Own Attachment Style

When you suffer from attachment issues, you naturally notice that your ability to have good relationships with those around you gets harder. You will discover that you will ultimately see that the relationships you develop are harder than ever to stay on target. Your relationships that you live are entirely sculpted by childhood—that much is undeniable.

However, no rules in life dictate that you are stuck. What if you can identify the filter that is shaping the perceptions that you make? What if you can change those filters that you see the world through? What if you can change how you relate to people in hopes of having the ability to change the way that you are referred to others? If you were able to play your cards the right way, you'd realize the truth—that you are quite capable of having the ability to combat those scars from childhood. You'll learn to develop your secure attachments in the future, and in having the ability to do so, you will learn to be a whole new you that is a lot more capable than you ever would have given yourself credit for, which is very important.

Humans are adaptive—we can change ourselves. We can mold to suit our environments. We will find out how we will alter the way that we engage with the world. We will prefer to make it a point to change how we tend to approach people and situations.

Yes, our childhood will inevitably and permanently be a part of us, but we will learn to change our perceptions. We will learn to identify how we see the world so that we will alter the way we respond. You can learn what it will take to better yourself, and once you do this, you recognize that you are often successful in any healthy relationship.

Ultimately, we develop our attachment styles and live them out through our inner monologues—how we perceive ourselves and the world around us. We will take a look at how we feel and why we do the items that we do. When it comes right down to it, that inner monologue and people's internal filters determine everything. They determine what we do and the way we do it. However, they don't need to be permanent. We will take the time to rewrite them into something better. We will work with the way the human mind works, and that we can cash in on that connection of that ability to overwrite and control the way that we think to make sure that we will regularly fix the narratives that we feature.

In this chapter, we will be addressing just that—we will be considering why our attachment styles hold a lot of weight in the first place, then take a look at what we will do to change them. When it comes right down to it, you can create a new narrative in your life. You can develop new ways of handling the relationships with everyone around you, and in doing so, you will discover what it will take to make sure that you can make that progress you are trying to find. Rather than continually reenacting the same behaviors and patterns you lived through as a toddler, you can change them.

## Unconscious Beliefs

Thoughts, feelings, and behaviors are learned early, and even though you are unaware of the connection between them, they still work in the same manner. Your mind has evolved to possess the potential to learn automatically—to be able to create the required connections and patterns to make it plastic. However, if you are not paying attention to the present process, you will realize that your brain's plasticity is often problematic. Yes, it is beneficial for us to be able to learn through experience, which is what happens. However, your mind can fall victim to the present over time— your mind can unintentionally concede to those patterns when they are unhealthy or unbeneficial, and you learn to live with them.

Think of this example: Imagine that you had a terrible experience involving cats. Perhaps one jumped at the back of your head, thinking that your hair was a toy, and you got scratched up badly as a toddler. As a result, you are now scared of cats. Is that normal? Not really. Is it healthy to be scared of one of the most common house pets that you will meet going about your day? Not at all—many households have them. However, anyone would say that it is understandable that you could be scared of them.

Similarly, you learn from those first relationships you foster and the early relationships you have with your parents. You bond with your parents first, which relationship sets the stage for every single one that you have afterward. If your parents aren't responsive, why would you ever think that people could be? If your parents are tired of ensuring that your relationships are secure, why would you think that those other relationships might be secure as well? While you may be too young to acknowledge these patterns as they play out early in your childhood and as you develop these expectations and assumptions, they are essential to ascertain in adulthood.

You may not have recognized them initially, but as you learn to see them, you will see that there are endless ways for you to work out not only what to expect but also how you can change them.

These ideas that you learn early are your beliefs regarding relationships, and they will create the connection patterns that you fall under as you age. You will see that the way you choose to interact with people depends on those in your infancy. Do you lack trust in people? Someone important to you may have let you down as a toddler. Do you prefer not to become involved with people in relationships? It is possible that you just don't like them. You learn early to make those quick judgments of the world around you so that you can rest on them when they matter most. Your experiences shape everything else, and your mind is meant to make generalizations that it follows based on those past experiences.

We are creatures of both nature and nurture; however, so keep in mind to a point, your personality and attachment styles are based on nature also. We tend to be avoidant, for instance, or the tendency to be attached. However, it is through nurture that we come to justify the trends that we have. If you grew up in a home where your parents regularly left you alone, you'd have a problem. You almost certainly never learned that you could count on your parents to guard you and keep you safe.

## The Connection Between Your Beliefs And Thoughts

When you have certain beliefs, they are always coloring your thoughts. Everything that you do, in the background, goes to be based on those unconscious habits that you have learned and developed. You know that you can't, for instance, trust your parents, which distrust inherently colors everything else that you do. That inherent distrust causes you to choose how you engage with people. It changes the way that you tend to make decisions. It causes you to think in very specific manners, which will directly influence everything else also.

Ultimately, the unconscious understandings that you have will always color the thoughts that follow. You know not to touch the pot on the stove because it is hot—that is because you have the assumption that it is. You know that pots on the stove are usually hot then you stay back from them. This is often because you learned that pots are hot that you should not touch them. Do you need to consciously remind yourself that the pots on the stoves could also be hot? Probably not—we learn effectively.

We have developed the capacity as humans to allow us to use unconscious thoughts; we don't need to be thinking as we navigate through life. We learn that some things are simply things and that we react accordingly. In terms of relationships, this means that you have an unconscious understanding that relationships are painful or relationships aren't inherently beneficial. This is often just how the mind works—when you have unconscious thoughts, you don't need to waste time deciding what to do or when to do it. You merely respond habitually, so you are not constantly wasting cognitive resources on determining how you ought to respond at the instant.

That means that the inherent beliefs you develop throughout your childhood become those unconscious thoughts; they become thoughts that tell you what to think of the way to behave. They are there to make sure that you can respond in life to save lots of time and psychic energy, but which will even be problematic. Of course, you will think that you will never know what it takes to overcome them if you have got these unconscious thoughts. If they are unconscious, they ought to be, by definition, outside of the realm of accessibility for you, right? Well, there are ways in which you can work to beat them. It takes time and energy, but you can do it, and we are going to be discussing that shortly.

## The Cycle Of Thoughts, Feelings, And Behaviors

Thoughts, feelings, and behaviors are continuously linked together. They endlessly cycle around themselves, influencing what you are doing, how you feel, and the way you think that. Consider it this way—

when you think that cats are scary, you will feel scared when you see a cat. When you feel scared, you will behave in very specific ways, according to feeling afraid.

You might attempt to run away. You may get aggressive as your fight instinct beats out the flight. You will make it a point to avoid the cat that you see in the corner. Regardless of how it is that you prefer to behave, your behavior only further reinforces your thought. If you avoid the cat because it is scary and nothing happens because you avoided it, your mind takes that to make the right decision. Your mind responds as if avoiding the cat is why things worked in the first place.

However, meaning that future interactions with the cat also will be limited in that manner. You will feel even more justified in fearing cats, meaning that you will never recover from it. What does this translate to when you consider your interactions with people in relationships, then?

The answer is simple: when you are in a relationship with people, you will always be using those self-same understandings that you developed through your childhood. You will use the same lens to look at every relationship that you ever had with your parents. If you learned early that your parents couldn't be trusted, you will probably have that very same approach when it generally involves your relationships. You'll discover that you cannot believe that your parents will support you; you will see that in time. The way your parents treated you and the attachment pattern you picked up will directly influence how you then engage with every future relationship.

Imagine that you are anxious-avoidant; for instance — you have learned that you haven't any real support in the relationships you have. You are so used to feeling such as you can't properly trust your parents to be aware of your needs, so you assume that your partners won't be responsive either. You approach things, believing that you will be guilty whenever you have a problem or can't trust your partner to assist. You then refuse to believe your partner, and what happens next? Your partner seems like your lack of trust is insulting or problematic. Your partner, if healthy, is going to be annoyed that you don't trust them. It is essential for there to be a solid foundation of trust in your relationships, and without it, how are you able to ever hope to relate to those around you properly?

When you make it clear that you won't trust your partner, you will probably quickly discover that they are unwilling to put up with that. You will find out that your partners won't want to interact with someone who will inherently afflict them or who isn't willing to be trustworthy. After all, trust is everything. Once you lack that trust, you run into a new problem; you run into the matter that they feel pushed away. You will find that your partner will leave you for that lack of trust alone, and as a result, you will feel entirely justified in having never trusted in the first place. After all, the act of being left would have happened anyway. You'd feel rejected even as readily, you tell yourself. Is it true? Who knows—relationships do fail sometimes, but let's be real here? The matter was a lack of trust. The lack of confidence is what led to the dissolving of the whole relationship. As a result, the lack of trust was the matter that you needed to avoid all along.

When it comes right down to it, then these unconscious thoughts will naturally shape everything you are doing. If you were to shift the thought process to be positive; instead, you'd see some very different results at the end of the day. Negative thoughts will nearly always breed negative relationships and negative consequences, and in fact, those negative results directly encourage the way you interact with the world.

## Overcoming Unconscious Beliefs

Because it is those negative thoughts that are at the basis of your problems, and in this case, it is the negative thoughts that you have developed surrounding attachments, you will start to work to fi the matter. Once you know that at its best, you can reduce all of your problems right down to the way that you think, you will see that there are natural ways in which you can shift what went on. You will learn what it will take to change up those thoughts so that you can better yourself. You will learn to beat those unconscious biases.

Being able to beat those beliefs in the first place is one of the most common treatment types that you can encounter when it involves psychotherapy. You will especially find that many of the prominent kinds of cognitive therapy, like cognitive-behavioral therapy, will have a huge influence on having the ability to change your thoughts. This is often to make sure that you are keeping up with people who will better for you. You will learn to challenge your unconscious beliefs that you have so that you can begin to correct the behaviors. Once you can find any of the unconscious beliefs that are highly problematic, you will find out what it will take to make sure that you stop giving in to those beliefs that hold you down.

Overcoming your unconscious beliefs requires that you learn the basics of the matter first, and this needs self-reflection. What is it that is controlling you? Why do you feel so influenced to behave in these ways regularly? What is it that keeps you down? What causes you to feel like you can't move toward the actions that you got to perform? Why is it that you struggle?

Think about it—what is the common problem you have had in every relationship you have had? For the most part, you will probably find that if you struggle in relationships, you either feel like your needs are unimportant and, therefore, not worth mentioning, or you feel like you can't trust those around you. You want first to find out the basis of your problem, often from childhood, impacting you so severely now.

Remember, insecurity in relationships and attachment is caused by not having the safety you need in childhood. Anxious attachment, for example, is typically created due to never getting needs met as a toddler. Ambivalent attachments are caused by learning that they can't express needs in the least or are going to be rejected so that they learn to completely suppress those needs rather than remaining close to their parents or caregivers.

When you recognize that ultimately, one of these issues is what caused the entire problem with those adult relationships that you pursue and find fail, you will be able to find out what to do that will assist you to beat those problems. Find out first what the problem is. Do you feel like you are not lovable? That's not the case—you are perfectly lovable and not responsible for your parents and their behaviors. Do you feel like your needs are irrelevant? That's not the case either—your feelings matter, and your needs matter also.

Effectively, to beat those biases, you need to work out what the problem is in the first place, then you need to change the way you address things.

## Rewriting Your Narrative and Changing Your Attachment Style

That brings us to this chapter's ultimate point: Rewriting your narrative to change your attachment style. We all carry inherent biases. We all carry around these inner stories that we use to look at everything that we do. We all mean we behave in these ways for a reason, and we make them a part of who we are. Imagine what your story would be for a second. How would you describe your life?

For some, they will write something like:

My life has been a continuing scramble. My dad was too drunk to even care much about what I do, and forget him ever having a meaningful conversation with me. He would come back from work and crack open that first drink and drink all day long. My mom was too preoccupied with her misery to ever really open up to me. When expressed, I quickly learned that my very own needs only ever added to her stress, so I learned that I could exclusively believe one person: Myself. I prefer it that way. It is often a little lonely sometimes, but be real here—when I only count on myself, nobody can let me down. I understand why my dad drank a lot now. Life is lonely, and you can't trust anyone anyway.

What do you notice in that story? Let's break it down—you can see that the individual wrote their story with a stress on their father's alcoholism. They never were able to have their own needs addressed because one parent was too incapacitated to take care of them while the other was too stuck in their own self-pity to do anything to change things. This meant that, even early, having needs that needed to be met was an immediate problem, and therefore, the individual stopped bothering even to try. What is the purpose if you will just be rejected anyway?

That narrative is extremely telling; in the narrative, you see someone that is stuck. You see someone who learned not to trust early and learned that their own beliefs were problematic to possess generally. This means that they are not going to be open or maybe expressing their needs. However, you can learn to change that narrative into something more beneficial.

That narrative can become respectable, which will be recognized for what it is—a testament to the human's desire to survive.

How much change after you alter your narrative, you may wonder? What kind of effects can reframe things that actually have? Consider this anecdote for a moment:

My parents let me down a lot. They weren't really there for me, so I learned that I had to believe in myself. I taught myself that I didn't want to be my parents—I didn't want to be the drunkard or the emotionally damaged individual. I didn't want to be so inherently broken that I couldn't love or trust. I took everything that I learned in my childhood and altered myself. I refused to involve myself with that. I refused to permit myself to fall under those habits, so as soon as I could, I left, and that I worked on myself. I had some bumps in the road here and there, but really, I'm growing and bettering myself every day.

Would you think that those are the narratives of the same person? They can be. Once you shift your focus to rewrite that narrative, removing the blame for the past, you will begin to change the way that you interact with future partners. You are not broken. You are not undeserving love. You are not guilty of the failures of your parents.

We all need to be loved and nurtured. We all need to be cherished and cared for. However, we don't always get the parents that we deserve. Life isn't fair, and sometimes, people get a life that is not fair either. However, you are what you create of your situation. Are you going to take the experience of getting bad parents and let it ruin everything, or are you willing to make it a point to change yourself? Are you willing to do better?

Challenge those negative thoughts.

Defeat those inner biases that you are unworthy or undeserving.

Remove the stigma from yourself and release the blame of your childhood.

Remember, you never asked to be born—your parents chose to bring you into the world, and since they did, it had been their responsibility to nurture and look after you. If they did not do so, you can't take the blame. You were not responsible for the behavior of adults.

When you start to abandoning those negative beliefs and appearance at how you have become a far better person over time, you will fix yourself. You will work on your perceptions of the world. You will learn to see that you aren't actually as broken or damaged as you will initially think. You deserve that respect, and only you will provide it to yourself.

# Understanding Your Partner in Distress

Throughout this all chapter, I'm getting to uncover some ways you can start to understand your partner. I want to let you know that this chapter is meant for people that are lovers of an anxious person. If that is you, you have to recognize the very fact that you need to understand your partner before you can fix their anxieties. It is weird, and it is going to be demanding.

Dobbs, a psychologist, said something about anxious people that you need to listen to. What is it? They get upset, they don't really know why, and they expect their partner to understand. So, you see where your job is. They have no idea what is wrong with them, and they want you to understand. Isn't that insane? Still, they' are right. Whether or not they have an idea or not, it is your job as their lover to save them. It is why you are both together. So, you have got to do it!

Brighten up! It is a hellacious task, but I'm going to show you how to get it done here. It is a reasonably long list. But that ought to be excellent news. I need you to make sure that regardless of how severe your partner's anxiety is, there is a way around it, and you are going to get that way here. You need to apply what seems appropriate in your relationship and let your friends use the rest. Shall we see them now? Let's do it!

## Be Willing To Do It

As the saying goes, making up your mind before you begin is a sacrifice package component. If you are going to help your partner out of their anxiety, you'd need to make a long queue of sacrifices. Making up your mind has to top that list due to the complicated nature of humans. Unlike forest animals, humans get frustrated and give up easily, but you will hold on for a little time longer if your mind is all made up to do something. Nothing comes easy-breezy. You would possibly assume you will easily help this person since it is your partner, but you ought to know that anxiety cares little about partners; in fact, it can tempt an anxious person to inform you it is over.

From years of empirical notes, I'd tell you that it is easy to help people with their finances, you can go to a bank and get loans, and you can help them when their health is weak or have a social boost. But psychological assistance is not mollycoddling. It'd be a little easier if your partner knows he needs help, and he is going to offer you an opportunity to help, but that is not how it works with anxious people. They are not fine, but they think the world needs fixing, not them.

Your anxious partner does not understand himself. He believes you have to understand him; he might agree he is not alright, but that is not to say he will allow you to treat him like an insane patient (Cheer up! It will always look that way to all of them, whether you treat them like a prince or a psych). Some won't even agree that something is wrong with them. It is often as bad as trying to tug someone to the clinic when they think you ought to be the one seeing a doctor. It can get really messy.

So, the first job you have is to determine that voice in yourself. You have to make up your mind that no matter your partner's gripes, you will get them out of that eerie they are suffering. Have you made up your mind? Great. Next!

# Specialize In It

Now that your mind is all made up. It is equally important to give your decisions a good push with actions. Take a while to review how you will act out your choices in your relationship. Your partner has changed, and a lot of changes need to happen too. You will have to show more care and attention than you used to. Whatever you choose to do at any time, let your compass be the will to get them out of anxiety.

By way of illustration, you have a partner who loves eating out with you, but all of a sudden, she is no longer interested. Your job isn't to prevent tugging at her for dinners because she seems to dislike it; your job is to return home with a crazily long list of the most recent foods in town. You now have the responsibility of sharing with her your fantasies about how you'd make a mess at the net dinner and crank up everyone to tease you two.

Give it your best. You have got to make your partner smile and remain interested. You will be unable to tell why she is anxious from the beginning, but if you focus on helping her, you will find out what makes her nervous and unwilling in the first place. It is crucial to recollect that you needn't change your lives completely because you are willing to help her, which may even pull her farther from you.

Instead, search for how to blend your focus. I'm going to tell you about an old client in the next illustration. You ought to be able to tweak a number of your habits like her. You ought to also make sure that your reaction to whatever she does isn't upsetting. Don't make the error of telling your partner you are trying to help, except if she feels that she needs some help, and she or he is asking you for it. Humans are egoistic. You won't let anyone push you around, either.

If your partner's anxiety arose from jealousy, it helps to lightly avoid or reduce interactions with people that would end in her envy. If it is something else, see if you can avoid that too. Nonetheless, don't attempt to fix yourself for her. A balance in everything is important. You both need to understand that there are no perfections; you only learn to tolerate some things.

# Be Calm

Okay, the relationship is getting jumbled up and confusing, right? The only sane person here is you. No kidding, your partner isn't insane, but his thoughts are clustered by his anxiety that leaves you because the only one that remains okay in the relationship. You have to act that way all the time. Even sometimes that he gets you infuriated and worried, calmness is your keyword.

As Dorothy Hans, a psychologist, has acknowledged, an anxious person isn't relaxed at all. They are uncomfortable, and they may need to yell, cry, or do nasty things at any moment. You will agree with Dorothy if you think about some of the days you were anxious yourself. For instance, how you felt when a Russian dog tried to mess with you.

There is an opportunity that your partner drives out of the garage and head straight into an ocean. Why? She is feeling a complete surge of anxiety. You certainly don't want to provoke and let her do anything like that, but you possibly would if you keep yelling at her. Don't say I didn't warn you.

She might not even go out to the car or rupture a vase. She might pick a chair and break the PC, that is, if she isn't breaking your nose or shattering the relationship. The reaction of an anxious person is decided by whatever got her on her nerves, and yes, whatever you tell her.

I love to reference one of my clients whenever I mention calmness. She handled her husband's anxiety in a way that inspires everyone who has an anxious partner. She is Meg, and she got married to Henry a few months into their courtship. He didn't seem odd initially, but she soon realized that there had been times he was uncomfortable.

They might be having a good time before she left home with him, but shortly, she would notice he was depressed when she called him at work. She couldn't imagine what was initially happening until they began to have more outings together. They attended parties and sightsaw tourist centers. He was with her at a couple of cinemas too; there, she noticed the strange things she had feared about him.

Once in a while, he would look gloomy and tired of what was happening around him. He would seek an excuse to use the restroom and hang out there for long hours. He would snap if Meg tried to ask why he took that long, and he would look sullen as he stared around the party, that is, if he decides to choose a seat eventually.

At long last, she realized he was anxious about something. She watched out for the days he reclined into a weird mood. He was always able to snap and get far away from that environment, and she realized that he was frightened of crowded places. She would hold him close at that point and tell him how much she loved him; she would tell him tales that he had told her some times. They might take a walk around the crowded places, and shortly enough, he began to melt and relax in mild crowds. He worked in a large office where countless offices were exactly why he was always cold over the phone. It'd have gone awry if she snapped back at him, but she understood and made something of their relationship. He loved her more and remained glued to her.

Can you interrelate her actions to your life? You will be surprised to know that you can remain calm no matter what happens. Regardless of how much you feel that urge, you do not need to raise your voice or snap at them. You furthermore may not need to change your life for them. Remember how Meg didn't stop going out because it made Henry awkward? She only found how to ease his distress.

## Give Them an Opportunity at their Blank Box

Have you noticed that you have gotten a blank box too?

I am talking about the moments when you don't want to think or speak to anyone. They are the days you yearn to do nothing aside from sitting and looking straight at the space and watch. You remember the moments you only want to be far away from everything. You are not happy or sad. You are not even crying or laughing. You need to be yourself. You wish to know nothing about the world and its significance. You'd be sitting right before a TV, and you'd see nothing of the comedy series. The blaring music doesn't get to you either. You see and listen to nothing at all. Moments like these happen in everyone's life repeatedly. It could happen in the car or at work, and you will not be shocked to know that it will happen more to an anxious person.

A psychology writer, Thieda Henry, points out that a blank box is a common feature of anxiety. Your partner might slip into such moments now then. You will feel the urge to jerk them out and stop them from thinking, but they are probably not overthinking; they are just proving what you already know, they are anxious.

As much as you feel that fire in your belly, you want to spare no effort to control it. This is often your partner's moment. It is his reflection spree. He has just hit the push button, and you want to let him be. I'm trying to pin down a point. Whenever your partner slips into anxiety, don't interrupt him or her for any reason. It is wrong to slide into the blank box with them, too, so don't attempt to get into their mood or see things the way they see it; neither is it commendable to jack them out of it by force. What to do? Stay away from it like you didn't know, get engrossed in other exciting things.

# Read the Maps

How much do you understand communication? It is time to pay more attention to your partner's signals. have you ever noticed? Humans communicate beyond the tongue and teeth. We send signals in every way we will. Our actions in situations, reactions to cases, expressions, and body language are enough signals for a keen listener to decode. They are media that pass factual information. It is possible to tell a lie with your words, but your actions and expressions are enough to give you away.

You need this level of understanding in your general relationships. You will understand people more if you learn to decode their other languages. You can even tell the facts that they are not letting out. If this will help you make casual interactions, can't it do a lot more in your relationship? Frankly, it can!

Your partner isn't just another person. You will fare fine if you can't read what others are saying; you will survive well if you know little about what people express with their bodies, but you can't get far in a relationship without comprehending your partner. You need to understand her beyond what she says.

What does she wish to do or say? What does it mean when she twitches their nose, frowns on her face, or rolls her eyes? What is she saying when she sighs? These body expressions have different meanings for everybody, and your partners should be as clear as a glass to you.

That way, you will be able to understand her pretty much, even her silences. She could be unwilling to speak or show you signs that she is troubled, but if you know her pretty much, something about her will give her away. There has to be one thing she stopped doing or started. Does she wish to sit for chitchats? Is she the one that wouldn't miss a show or sleep without country music?

There has to be a sign, work it out! The same thing applies if your partner is male. He is probably right that you should understand him even when he doesn't understand himself. Don't you think?

If your partner likes to dance on the days, he isn't doing anything, dumping his pastime could be a strong sign. He might be the type who always has some terrific words for your cooking skills. The moment he starts to chop the cackles, you ought to know there is something awkward. I have to remind you that these signs aren't absolute tips that could be anxiety. They might mean other things. You need to acknowledge the sign before you opt that anxiety is in the game. We talked about the signs already.

## Duck-Shove Complaints

'You tousled again!', 'you let it slip!' 'That mistake was egregious!'

Hurling complaints is a fast way to deteriorate the entire relationship. Naturally, everyone hates to listen to complaints from people. We hate it when people hurl words that make us feel as if what we did was a shipwreck. You hate it too. Most people don't mind being corrected. But you need to do it in a welcoming and less criticizing manner.

As it is, your partner is jittery already. You will only drive the relationship downhill by bulldozing your partner with words. She is upset already, and she or he will welcome whatever would fuel her fury; you will see that. Complaining never makes anything better, so you have to make sure whatever you say is casual and calming enough.

Now, I have to make a point clear. You can't put up with all of your partner's behavior just because he seems to worry. No! It is wrong. Meaning you are encouraging him to worry or, at the smallest amount, pretends to be so that you will always agree with him. Believing him can also make him feel like he is battling a severe problem, and you\ are not willing to argue because he's neurotic. Let's put it straight. There are several things that you don't want. I can't be specific because you can accept things and that I can't, the other way around.

Nonetheless, your partner has to know what you don't want. You need to confirm two things; first, whatever you say doesn't sound like an interrogation. You won't get much if you present your request like an interrogation where they need to defend themselves, attack you, or find some alibi. All you ought to put to him is a suggestion.

Next, make sure that it is not an attack. If you will tell him to stop drinking, for example, you would possibly start with, "honey, I think drinking might not be the answer. You will be able to think clearer and find out how if you are not drunk."

It sounds more like a suggestion than a protest or an attack, right? That is the spirit.

## Empathy

Empathy is one of the essential skills you need at this moment. What does it even mean? It refers to the power to place you in the shoes of people and understand exactly what they are passing through. It is about seeing things how someone sees them, feeling their pains, sadness, and joy with them.

Is that even possible? Sure! You have the potential to know people if you listen with an open mind. You need to hide your prejudices, suggestions, and beliefs. Then hear them as if you got no idea what they were saying. Listening isn't all. You ought to also imagine you are in their situation. Think in their shoes and consider the choices you have. See the possible reasons you would possibly have done what they did too. This way, you can train yourself to be empathic. That is, understand people better without toting your personal opinions.

Now that you are empathetic, you will get to apply it with your weird partner. Her recent behavior doesn't deserve it, but she is your partner, and you can't give up on her. If your partner is worried because he is not wealthy enough, for instance, you can show him empathy. You can convince him that you know what it feels like to have extra money, but one doesn't need to be aroused over not having it. Imagine you are calmly sitting beside him and trying to way that to him. Isn't it a satisfying sight? Yes, it is bait, and your partner can bite it from you.

It is always soothing to understand that despite being clearly misunderstood by the world, someone understands you. that somebody isn't just anyone, in fact. It is your ally, your companion! Being empathetic to my cause is the easiest way to my heart, your heart, and anyone's heart. You will only need to remember that as you concentrate on getting your partner's points, you do not get swamped in depression with her. You are the doctor, the one with the cure. The infection shouldn't get to you.

## Set To Blend

Correcting others is a job that we are all good at. We will tell when something isn't right and that we instantly want it fixed. But our way of asking people makes it difficult for them to yield to our corrections, except if they are people that haven't any choice but to listen to us.

In the case of your lover, he is your partner, not your junior colleague. As such, it'd be hard to tell him anything and expect him to yield. He might, due to love. But that is no guarantee because he is anxious. You will certainly feel the urge to change your partner. You have to look into his face and tell him he has to stop cringing before a dog. You want to nap at her that her jealousy is entirely unfounded, and she must stop, among other belongings you want to finish directly.

As much as you would like to ask them to change, you should know that trying to force them is a very wrong thing. Your partner could be anxious against her will. That makes it hard to hope for a few voluntary changes in her. It is okay to suggest some improvements to her. But you can't change her at that instance. Instead, seek to blend her state with the present situation instead.

For example, if your partner has chosen to prevent attending parties because parties are crowded, don't expect her to go back to an evening ball just because you talked to her about it. Instead, start by inviting her to less crowded parties where they could meet a lot of individuals they are conversant with. Their anxiety is often stemmed that way. What else did your partner recline from? Find how to compromise. They can't change, and you're not getting off their back. You're blending.

## Do It For Love

Staying with an anxious person is often the worst experience of your life. He doesn't think he is doing something he has to quit. He thinks you are the problem instead, and he is not even able to say it. His mood swings can leave you perplexed. You ought not to be surprised that you will receive thumbs down for many of your efforts. Who cares? He'd ask you.

From the researches of Dorothy Hans in 2018, it became clear that several marriages break because a partner threw their lover's affection to the dogs out of hysteria. He was worried about other things, but he stopped picking your calls. He stopped spending time with you, and he cares little about what you both had together. It might be a she too. In the end, their partner ends up calling it to quit out of frustration.

Soon after the breakup, the anxious partner realizes that the partner he ditched was someone he couldn't do without. He tries to get back to the connection, but it becomes a broken mirror that they can't put together. This could be what happened together with your 'ex,' or perhaps, the reason your ex called it quits with you.

I remember telling you that as a non-anxious fellow, you are the only sane person in the relationship, and you want to act precisely that way. You are not alleged to treat your partner as insane. You can't hold them for everything they assert or do either. They're tense at the instant. If you offer them that point, they are sure to come around and apologize. This is often why you shouldn't interrupt their blank box- moments. Be quick to recollect that your relationship is relying on you. "True love is selfless. It is prepared to sacrifice"- Sadhu Vaswani j.

## Don't Quit On Them:

Have you read through everything I even have said all day? Then, you ought to have seen an undeniable fact; you can't hand over on your lover. They are sure to be weird and filled with surprises. But Maria Bastida tries to plea:

There will be challenges along the way. There will be times that you will feel as if they don't just understand, and you'll feel like you ought only to stop loving the person and walk away. Please, don't get away when she tries to push you away; she doesn't mean to do that, dear.

Did you read her last sentence? It is one of the complicated sentences you will ever hear. My partner pushed me away; what else am I supposed to do, hold her close like I'd die if she doesn't return? Crazy, but yes. That is precisely what you are supposed to do.

There is no reason you have to spend a day trying to find someone to like or return your love. There is no reason you have to keep jumping here and there in a relationship. It sometimes takes time, but as long as you remain faithful and steady with your partner, they discover you are the only one that ever showed them love, and they head right back to you.

I must state this without mincing words; you have to give them breathing space once they need it. You have to walk away from them once they clamor for loneliness. You have to be quick to ascertain when they really don't want you in their lives but you ought to remember, among other things, giving up on an anxious partner isn't among the best hundred options.

## Be Helpful

Do you remember the last time you were scared to the bones because a Rottweiler (that is a dog breed) was waiting to pounce on you and tear you apart? How would you feel if someone nippily showed up and broke its neck (no offense to vegans)? Wow, thank God! Isn't it?

It is the same case whenever you are anxious about other things. Whether your anxiety is about phobias or feelings, you will always wish someone would promptly show up, change the game, and provides you a hand. Foreseeably, your partner needs that hand and support, too; they have someone to assist with a number of their odd jobs.

They wish someone would help call the laundry, order the meals, and do other boring assignments for them. Don't be shocked, they could be willing to spend up their energy on these boring assignments too. That is not something you ought to discuss with them. If they need to do it, just let them!

The most important point here is that you are here to help your partner and offer some support. Your partner may prefer to tell you or not, but there is always something you can do to assist her. Depending on the kind of hysteria she is battling. If it feels right, call her office to inform them that "she's not pretty good, and she or he won't be exposure at work today." It might impress your lover that you got her the time off but make certain that she wants before you are trying it. Sometimes, she needs you to ask an old friend, a counselor, a doctor, or someone special. Recognize these blanks, and give it a reasonable effort.

## Ferrule their Flaws

Hey, we all have flaws, isn't it? Yeah, we all do, but one of the exciting packages of affection is that you don't see their flaws once you love someone. No! you really see the issues, but your love for them neutralizes the imperfections like they don't even matter. Something similar is occurring to your lover too. They know you are a nut in the head, but they prefer to persist with you, regardless.

Now that it is all gone awry, you ought to know that your lover will add more flaws than ever. She will pile numerous flaws that you start to recall the old ones and feel a strong hatred for her. You begin to wonder why you saw all of those things and stuck with her; you start to think it makes much sense to drop her at this stage, but as far as you have your flaws too and she chooses to remain with you, dumping her will remain a bad idea.

Dumping her would mean that you cannot hang onto her at bad times; you want to measure and merry. Love, because the parish says, is "for better or worse." We already agreed you'll step aside if you have to. We hinted that you don't need to put up with all of their behaviors. You can put what doesn't please you to her, so she is going to catch on. Your options are enough to help you look over her flaws; dumping her is a screw-up idea. Dumping him is additionally wrong!

Rather than drop her, think about using any of the choices in this last paragraph, ask her about what she is doing wrong, and make sure you avoid speaking in provoking manners. You certainly have the right to be expressly mad at her, but your first focus is to get her out of that anxiety, do you remember? Impressive! That's exactly why you'll not regard her misbehaviors as what's it yet. Just ask her about what has got to change.

You have to take note. Your partner must not, from your tone, detect that she has been doing one of the most horrible things anyone should. You are certainly getting to get that chance to tease her later, but now is the wrong time. You are here to get them out, focus!

The bottom line is that you shouldn't make your partner feel bad about their flaws. Ask them about whatever seems wrong but be moderate and constructive.

## Retain the Connection

Maintaining connection is an efficient way to understand an anxious partner. As I have proved earlier on, a nervous partner might try to get a break from everything, including you. Suppose your partner is affected by a terminal illness, for instance. In that case, she might become nervous and begin to believe she would die soon; she might begin to give up on the world around her, she might stop hanging out at parties, refuse to take her medications, or stop playing at the court. She is going to withdraw from the connection too naturally. Nobody in her circle will understand her, and she or he knows that. Consequently, she feels unwanted and tired of whatever happens outside the world, plus your relationship.

If you understand her before that moment, you will not find it hard to note that change. You will be able to guess the matter she is grappling with, but you still need to retain the connection if you can't tell what the matter is. Whether she tries to chop ties or stay aloof, you're the closest one that can help her.

So, don't quit on her, maintain your old manners with her, ask her as you have always done. Offer her good food, romance, comedy, sex, and everything you used to have in the relationship. Your efforts can help her to see that she still has you. She is going to likely consider you a confidant and open up to you soon.

Trust me, this will work for a 'he' or 'she' partner. We all want someone who wouldn't give up on us, regardless of how crazy we are. What's more, psychology schools report that anxious people want the attention they are desperately running from, you do not want to forget that.

## Listen

This list is not sealed without this.

Have you ever tried to listen to an anxious person? Frustrating.

You can hardly make head or tail of whatever they are telling you. You'll thrust aside whatever they assert because it makes little sense, and it isn't very pleasant. You'll be right, but discarding their words is one of the most expensive mistakes you'll make.

You may not concentrate, but their fears, their feelings, and the source of their anxiety are always embedded in what they say. Could we take an example?

"I am through with this relationship! You all suck. Nobody bloody cares! You are a liar!"

If your partner yelled this way while she was upset, you would likely thrash everything she says. You will probably feel she was only confused or upset about many things. What you probably did not notice was that she had told you everything you needed to understand. Are you wondering how? Here is it.

If she had just called you a liar and she'd just aid that nobody actually cares, then she has just been failed by someone she trusted; she has always had the gut that you weren't reliable. This may flow from the way you associated with other girls around her, or she just heard rumors that you are fooling around from whoever-it-is.

She might still lollygag around because she loves you, and a part of her might be sure that the rumor wasn't valid, but she was anxious that you would dump her, which is precisely what she has told you.

Revealing, isn't it? It sure is.

Let's not even mention the other signs. If you learn to listen more to what your anxious partner says, you will decide what seems wrong and find out how to help them.

## Acknowledge Your Feelings

I am going to wrap this long session off with this.

You deserve as much care as your partner does. You are only giving them more because they are not in their sound minds. This could not rule out a fact, however. You are a person, and you have feelings too, you want never to stem your emotions for people, you ought to acknowledge what you think and make the best of it whenever.

Get angry when you feel angry. You are feeling angry, and there is no reason you ought to hold back all the angry voices in your head. Walk away when you are urged to do it, don't hide your excitement, too. You need to make sure that you do not drive your partner up the wall as you acknowledge your feelings. Don't get too angry and flare up at your partner. Remember, you vowed to yourself that you were going to get your partner out of their anxiety; that is a reason you ought not to vent your flames in their anxious face, regardless of the circumstances.

# Making Your Partner Understand You

Let's take a different look at everything, you need to help your partner understand you too. We have spent the entire last chapter trying to point out to your partner how to understand you. On the flip side, you have to assist them in understanding you also. If you are the anxious guy who thinks the world doesn't understand, the subsequent lines are exclusively for you. I'm never excluding the anxious woman in the relationship too.

Without mincing words, I have no doubts that you are sane, I don't doubt that there is nothing wrong with your head or mind. I also believe that you need to be understood no matter how anxious you are feeling, but I have to make you understand one reality; the whole world won't get you if you don't help us do it got to give us the signs. Or, how do you think your partner might get the message you are not passing?

Since you are keen on your partner and do not want the bond to break over anxiety, you must pass the message. Subsequent few lines are gathered from top psychologists and counselors. They were also collected from people that were formerly anxious and their partners. They are going to help you to twig the ways you can help your partner understand you. Are you able to uncover the mysteries about yourself? Well then, let's get to it!

## Don't Zero Your Mind

Do you know the error anxious people make all the time? They zero their mind. According to the American Depression Association, it is hard to understand people because they do not make it easy to understand them. They believe nobody can understand how they feel, and so, they are never willing to speak to anyone about it.

If you are depressed and locked away in your closet all day, there is no way anyone can give a hand or support you. You are not giving them a chance. In another case, you should not be locking yourself in your room, but you have made up your mind that you are talking to nobody. That is not so different from locking yourself up. Nobody can understand you that way.

According to empirical researches, anxious people zero their minds for several reasons. You already believe that no one will believe you, so you find it hard to take a sit anyone down and talk about it. Is that your fear? Oh. One more reason is that you assume everyone will think you are going nuts, but do you know what? Your reaction makes them think you are going nuts already, so it can't hurt to see more of your weird stories. If that's not it, you would possibly be suffering trust problems. You are unsure who to trust or who you shouldn't. It'd be that you aren't sure of the right words to use. You can't find the right moment, so you permanently zero your mind.

Regardless of why you decided to zero your mind, you ought to know that you aren't just hurting yourself. You are equally hurting your partner and making no headway in your relationship. The essence of affection is to believe one another. It is to trust and support one another, so you have to make efforts to keep your mind open. Be ready to talk, be willing to express what you are feeling. Even if they will think you are insane, your partner deserves to share in your fears and anxiety. Don't zero your mind.

# Talk

Is your mind open? Great. The net task is to speak to your partner. I have to agree that this could be hard. You are sure to feel happy and sad at the same time, you will feel relaxed while an earthquake is occurring in your head, you will see a storm when everyone sees a comedy series on the TV, and every one of those makes can take over your spirit. They will make it hard to utter a word.

You will feel such an outburst that you might want to explode in your own world, but everyone seems normal, and they haven't any idea what you are thinking about. You would possibly even try to use some words, but you can't explain because your speech repertoire seems suspended. You can only stare because no words are coming.

This is how hard and sad you would possibly feel, but shall I repeat the law of affection to you? Whether in joy or sadness, you have to remain in-tuned with your partner in pain or pleasure. They have to understand how you feel; they have to listen to anything from you, anything that will tell them how you are feeling. They need to make certain you trust them even in adversity. These are cogent reasons you have to speak to them.

As I even have earlier acknowledged, it is impossible to speak sometimes, but when you get your voice, you want to make efforts to reach them. You have to allow them to understand what you are feeling and the way everything looks to you. As often advised by Wyatt M, you ought to ask them. You need to keep it straight and simple. If your lover asks you, for instance, "Honey, is everything fine?" you can roll your head to inform them no. You can tell them to spare you a while by gesturing with your palms, among other styles. The moment you can talk, leaving them brief words is enough. "I feel unsafe publicly. I will be able to talk once I feel better." "Something isn't right here, but I'm yet to work it all out," et cetera. Can you picture how you can manage to speak to your partner net time you are anxious? In many ways, I knew you'd do it!

## Exchange Love All The Time

Now here is a few sensitive information you have to deal with. Exchanging love is usually grand. You two can stay cozy in each other's arms and feed yourselves with everything, but that is when you aren't entangled in an imbroglio. The instant you have things that bother you a lot, you might care little about sharing the love. The only thing that pops up in your mind is your worry and thoughts of the way to escape from it.

I will agree it is hard, but there is always a way you can manipulate your mind with force. There is a way with which you can prompt your body to express love to your partner. I cannot recommend one because there are no general ones. You need to consider one yourself. You don't need to do it when you don't feel up to it. It'd be the last thing you have to do when you are upset, but as much as you feel no energy for it, you would like to struggle to do it.

It is an absurd thing on behalf of me to ask you, but it's one of the items you'd need to learn. Sharing love is the key to unity. You'll be unable to share as much as you used to, but a peck on the cheek or a hug in your shoddiest moments can do wonders. Try a smile in the face of adversity if that is what you can use. These mentions are examples. You'll decide how best to point out love, even in your circumstances. It helps reassure your partner, and it can hone what proportion they understand you. Appreciate your lover and prove that you care, regardless of the number of bombs bursting apart in your head.

## Leave The Trails

Do you want to help your partner understand you? Then, give them the clues!

There are not any more magicians. If there are, I'm tempted to assume that your partner isn't one of them. You know that too. For that reason, you only cannot expect any magic from them. What? Did you tell me you were expecting magic? Yes, you did! Right from the instant, you expect your lover to know you without leaving the paths; you expect him to do a lot of magic.

Most of the time, we all can decode unspoken words. The design on a person's face can tell you if they are scared to death or they hate you to the skies. They didn't say any of these things with words, but we hear them, as clearly as we might if that they had used their words.

When you want your partner to know you, you have to point it out, too, whether you say it or not. Your manner of showing it'd change again. There is no reason you ought to look or stare at your partner like a doll so that they could read your eyes and think. Actually, they will be unable to see more than the iris in your eyeballs. This is often why you ought to adopt the no-shoes-fit-all approach.

What does this mean? There's no general way to express all of your feelings. If you are anxious about trying something new, it'd be for several reasons. Majorly, you bought a ticket to the clinic the last time you tried a new diet; you would possibly be unwilling to inform your partner because he wasn't here the last time, you furthermore may don't want him to think you're thankless for the efforts he wasted by getting you something sweet. What to do? Give him the signs.

Let him realize that you are excited about the food from your behavior. You have to make him see that you look sick once you stare at the food too. He would soon realize that you were happy about his efforts. You only didn't like anything about the food.

This food fallacy is an illustration. There have gotten to be other ways you'll leave the paths. Considering that how you create your partner see things doesn't need to be the same as anyone else's ways.

# Appreciate Them

Do you remember you are the edgy one here? Your partner is neutral. She is also not in your head, so she isn't exactly sure how you feel. She will assume it had been the same you by all instincts and try to help you. You need to appreciate that help if you want them to understand you better. Confused?

Here is what I'm talking about; you and your lover began to go to a family friend. The instant you stepped into their garden, some ferocious-looking dogs met you. They were barking hard and charging at you two already, but you were lucky; your friend showed ahead of time. That made nothing better because you have a fanatical hatred for dogs. So, you were anxious all day, and you kept shaking, looking around to see if another dog would leap out of the kitchen.

Your partner seems fine after the encounter, but it had been clear to him that something isn't right with you. He is sure to move closer and ask you questions. 'Honey, is everything fine? What is the problem? What are you worried about?' and similar questions, do you have to scream at them? Wrong!

Appreciate him. He must know that you are glad he is worried about you. Thank him or rest on him with affection. It is one of the best ways you can handle your anxiety in your relationship.

Did I remember to mention that it is an illustration? Whether you seem jealous, have a sheer dislike for noise, or merely go over the board about anything, appreciate your lover. They need to see that you care.

## Talk

Shouldn't you talk at all? Aww. That is another mistake anxious people often make; it is okay to repeatedly get into a ghost mood. You only want to keep your head in your hands and stare at your toes; you do not even want to listen to or see anyone. It is okay to get into a blank box now, then, but something is wrong. Remaining blank!

You need at least one person in the world to understand you, no matter your situation. That person should be your life partner. It needs to be someone who's around you all the time, even in your bed.

You can hope that she will figure out what kicked you off-balance by reading your trails, but what if she can't? What if your partner is becoming too stressed to read the clues you are giving? You have to speak, darling; I have seen spectacular marriages enter shambles because the partners don't say things to each other. I have earlier acknowledged that it is okay to hit your blank box and that I need to put it in your mind that you are not staying in your empty box forever. You can feel the urge to speak once in a while. Once you are up to it, does it!

You may want to keep it short and straight. That is a true way to control yourself from spewing things that aren't necessary. It stops you from getting upset and getting all steamed up with your partner too. She loves you, and she or he doesn't need to be frustrated, right? Many ways.

You may also want to focus on the time you tell her. It'd be no good to inform her when she is totally uninterested in you and your oddness. She must know what's wrong, and she or he must realize it soon. So, tell her at the right time. g. Relive the beautiful times:

Relive the beautiful times? Yes! That's a trick I prefer to give to my clients whenever I detect diagnose them with anxiety. It works best for people whose anxiety stems from jealousy, insecurity, et cetera.

In the general pattern of our adult lives, we've all had some good pasts. We have had some good moments we treasure and a few sizzling experiences we can't recover from. Indeed, we had some not-so-impressive ones, too, but because the Briggs and Myers Foundation has proven, reliving your past can influence your present situation. What does that mean?

If you have had some terrible pasts, you will become sad and heartbroken when you remember that past. It might not even matter if you were excited before your memory picked on the past. The story is analogous on the flip side. You can lift your spirits by calling your good moments back to your mind. I prefer to offer an illustration even though it's going to never happen to you today.

Imagine you are in a jungle where it is just you and a few tigers. You have only one club in your hand, and you have no gun or magic to get you out of there. The tigers started wagging their tails when they saw you (dinner is set!), and majestically, they began to stride towards you. There is no escaping this, you can't take a flight because this is their territory. You have to fight before dying or find yourself in their belly without any resistance.

You kept your eyes on them as they strode closer, then a memory stuck in your mind; your mom is right there sitting on a chair, she was in tears as she asked you if you were going to revisit her. You promised her that you would do your best to return for her love. Your husband was also a few meters away, your daughter and your ally are struggling to wipe their tears, and you kept telling them you will breeze through for them. The vision wiped off as the tigers roared 100 meters far away from you. What would you feel as you roar up to face the Tigers again? Fear, anger, resolution to fight or die, what?

I am pretty sure you know how much hatred you'd feel at that moment. You'd feel as fierce as the tigers, and you'd be burning to eat them up yourself. That is how much the past can do to you!

That same way, you can wriggle out of your current circumstances if you relive your best moments. Whenever you feel your partner is not getting the hang of things, think about the past moments you had with them. Get inspired, and find out how best you can put it to them. That's love!

## Empathy

Empathy is the ability to know what other people are thinking about. We will agree you are the one going through things here, and there is no two-way to mention that you need that skill too. As much as you crave to be understood, people around you may need to be understood. It comes across as a person's feature. Whenever you need something from people, you would like to offer that thing too. For instance, if you need help from people, give it. You need love from people; share it. Now that you want to be understood by your partner seek to know them too.

How are you able to do it?

The first thing to do is to relax. An anxious person isn't a relaxed person. You are sure to be uncomfortable in one or two ways, but you can't move a step further if you can't pull your nerves together and think straight. You can retain as many of the other features you can't let go of but make sure you relax as much as you can. Make efforts to control yourself from beating a dead horse and spurring anxiety.

Then, be open. As I even have empathically stressed earlier, you have to be creative, entirely. You would like to prevent brooding about yourself and your worries. Check out your partner and see-through him. What could he see about you? How would you feel if this is often how you are bothered about him? What would you think that, how would you react? You have to make efforts to know him, as much as you equally want him to know you.

This way, you'll begin to see things from their perspective, even as very much like you would like them to ascertain things from yours. It will also become easier for you to speak to them. You can help them out of the mystery you threw them into. I will be able to spend one of the approaching chapters on empathy.

# This Can't Get Overboard

Is this anxiety going overboard? Good. Don't let that happen. You will lose an excessive amount of than you are prepared to lose if you let it get overboard. So, don't let it.

What does it mean to go overboard?

It means your anxiety is getting too complicated and uncontrollable. You are beginning to freak out aggressively. Your anxiety keeps going over the top, and it seems there's no answer. We are saying that it goes overboard when it's getting out of control, and you'll do nothing about it; then you'll start to disregard your partner and shut the world far away from you. You will always be scared and unable to relax. You will hurt your partner by your words and action, and that they will have little choice but to steer far away from you.

Often, this is what happens to anxious people that still love their partners. First, you are anxious, and you do not care to admit it. You think that something is wrong with everyone around you, plus your partner, and you see him or her as a nuisance. You begin to slam them and hurt them till they can't take it anymore. Then they involve divorce, and you blame them for walking away from you.

If you have broken things with your partner at any time, you will realize that this is often precisely what happened in your relationship. Now that you know, I strongly suggest you get your partner to read these lines and return to you. Why? Because true love can't be broken. It doesn't die. It finds how to stay alive and haunt you for the rest of your life. You don't need to be haunted. Work things out need like not fix anything:

Is your partner getting worked out because you are saying nothing to them? Allow them to see through you.

If you have a boyfriend who feels you are not happy with him, make sure he understands that he is not the source of your anxiety-if he's not. As long as your partner is loving and attentive, he is very likely to think he is the matter. He might start to think you are uninterested in him, you don't like something about him, or you prefer someone to him, which is why you are not willing to speak to him.

Ideally, he would be able to change anything about himself. He would want to hear what you don't like about him, the environment, or whatever he can change in the world for you. Oddly, there's nothing he can change.

So, instead of keeping him unsettled jittery, it helps to try to speak with him and help him understand that he needs not to fix anything. You are battling some tough times, and you can tussle with it pretty much.

## Be Willing To Compromise

I have to tell you this also. It is important to compromise in a relationship. Your partner is another one that has an entirely different mindset. She possesses a life, a mind, and a perspective of her own. It's practically impossible that you share the same perspectives in everything that matters. You prefer a bungalow, and he's dreamy for a flat, you care about green living, and the flowers mean nothing to her, you like vases or louvers, et cetera. Whatever it is that you don't agree upon, you need to learn to compromise. Your partner has to do it too. You can't both have your ways all the time.

In this situation, you have far more than trivial cases to stress about. You need to start showing your partner what doesn't work for you and what you can put up with. You may have to realize that there are certain things you'd need to put up with if you want to retain that relationship.

As a case in point, you have a partner who dances or pursues a career in the humanistic discipline. He is exposed to all or any shapes and sizes of attraction. Men and ladies would love him and need to possess him. If you're jealous, you can't find that exciting; the more he gets more limelight in his career. What to do? Are you going to ask him to quit his career because he loves you?

No way. It doesn't happen anywhere, honestly. You would possibly need to walk away from them, or you'd need to control your anxiety and obtain used to their lives. This partner is the love of your life, right? Then, you recognize the only choice you've got.

## Give Your Partner A Chance

Do you actually need to let your partner in on why you're all worked up and nervous? Then tell it straight to him. Let him understand that she is the reason you are upset. It is best to make her know the thing she did that sparked jealousy, anger, or unrest in you. 'Babe, you were hanging out with the lowlife down the road, and it still makes me sick.' Remember to keep your words short and straightforward.

You should also attempt to stress more on you and your roles than theirs. For instance, "I feel heartbroken. I'm not sure..." this way, you can avoid pointing fingers at them or making them feel guilty for your feelings. Remember, you will make nothing better by lamenting. You would like to resolve things, and you'll do it amicably. m. end up the cure:

What is the best answer to your current situation?

You might think you won't be reading this book if you knew, but I think that you realize it already. You have read over twenty pages in this guide. You have a good idea of what you or your partner might expect of every other. You can also take a quick guess at what sort of anxiety you are battling and your best answer.

You must have found out what got wrong together with your relationship as a result of anxiety. You may have seen how best to handle it. I'm getting to add some words nonetheless. The cure to most of our problems lies in our hearts. Be wanting to cure yourself and your appearance through your emotions. There has got to be something that calms you a lot.

It might be taking note of a bit of favorite music, watching polo games, racing, reading a completely unique, or anything. It's faster to make people understand you once you are clear about your situation. You'll even be able to recognize the best way or role your partner can play in your anxiety.

## Invite Support

Call for help! It's a surprise that a mean American can call the cops in but five minutes of experiencing a shock. I mean any sort of situation that threatens their physical wellbeing like an attack from a ruffian, robbery, inferno, et cetera. But a mean American never thinks they have helped, even if the fires of hysteria are burning their minds.

From the instant you have picked this guide, you are not a mean person. You now understand how people's minds work and the way they react, especially in relationships. You have to prove that by doing the right thing when necessary. The moment you think that you would like help, call out for help at the acceptable quarters. Do you think your partner can assist you by agreeing to relocate? Do you think she might try to talk to your neighbors about their dogs? Do you feel you both got to spend a while with the counselor? Call out for support whenever it's necessary. It is a superb way to help your partner have some idea what precisely might be going wrong in your mind.

Now spare me a second to answer an issue. Do you think your relationship might still lack some vitality despite applying all of those in your relationship? It just can't happen; the cure possesses to be here!

# Emotion-Focused Therapy (EFT) and Additional Practices

This chapter will explore the connection between traditional Emotion-Focused Therapy (EFT) and the additional practices that I have empirically found helpful in thousands of case studies. We will explore the connection between your attachment style, the core subconscious wounds in that attachment, and the traditional techniques practiced in EFT.

Emotion-Focused Therapy is a technique used to diffuse emotional distress. Developed by Gary Craig in the late 1990s, it pulls from a spread of therapeutic tools like neurolinguistic programming and Thought Field Therapy. It focuses on the notion that emotions are intended to be used as a guide which dismissing them can cause long-term psychological harm.

EFT focuses on three first concepts:

- — How emotions are produced
- — How emotions affect human functionality
- — How emotions are associated with thought and behavior

EFT examines how emotions are experienced physically, affect physiological functions, influence thinking, and impact behavior in the core concepts. By using EFT, a person can better understand their emotions and take away themselves from behaving emotionally instead of logically. By expanding on traditional EFT teachings and partnering them with attachment theory, you can better navigate conflicts and understand what your emotions try to inform you.

The practices outlined in this chapter are excellent for any attachment style;

However, they will be especially helpful for the Anxious Attachment, the Fearful- Avoidant, and the Dismissive-Avoidant. Since each of those attachment styles has unmet subconscious needs that are easily triggered, an approach that mixes the subconscious and EFT will help resolve disputes. Moreover, since competing needs are inevitable in any relationship, the approach outlined in this chapter will help guide us back to more positively oriented practices.

# Diving into Your Emotions

To illustrate how EFT works, the way to expand upon its traditional teachings, and how to work through attachment theory in conjunction with EFT, imagine that a conflict arises between two sisters. The younger sister, Emily, has an Anxious Attachment. The older sister, Julie, is a Dismissive-Avoidant. They are arguing over who gets to take the family car for the weekend. Emily wants to borrow it to go to a friend's cottage. Julie wants to use it to go into the town and visit her spouse. Remember that since they have different attachment styles, each of their core wounds is being projected onto the argument through the shape of various beliefs or stories about the circumstances. Emily fears that, without committing time and energy into her friendships, she risks losing her friends. Julie has recently gotten into an argument with her partner and has taken space over a previous couple of days to process the argument. Julie feels if she doesn't enter the town to resolve things, her relationship might be in trouble.

Different beliefs also will be projected onto their argument. Julie will withdraw from Emily when they argue to process her emotions. Emily will fear that she is losing her emotional reference to her sister and can plan to talk things through immediately afterward. Now that the argument between the two sisters is printed and their core wounds and beliefs are illustrated, we will explore what EFT would reveal about the circumstances and in which ways we will expand on traditional EFT theory.

## Identify What Feelings Were Present in the Conflict

In previous chapters, we outlined the importance of taking a moment to witness and identify the emotions that arise in conflict. This easy technique reactivates the neocortex and shifts our brains back to a logical state. According to traditional EFT, a person would question how their emotions were produced, what physical reaction these caused, and the way the emotions could influence future behavior.

Take a moment to acknowledge in which areas you are feeling your emotions in your body. If you are angry, maybe you are feeling tenseness in your fists. If you are nervous or anxious, maybe there is a pit in your stomach. Identify all the emotions that are present. The simple act of witnessing and inquiring will move you into a reflective state and out of a reactive state.

In Emily and Julie's case, each sister would feel various things in several areas due to their attachment styles. Emily would likely feel fearful and clingy toward Julie after the initial argument and should feel it in her stomach or chest. As a Dismissive-Avoidant, Julie would feel withdrawn and feel the frustration in her extremities as a result of her flight response. If both sisters were to require a flash to think about their emotions and where they're feeling them, they're going to shift in their brains into the cortex and neocortex and be better prepared to resolve the conflict.

Ultimately, the first step in traditional EFT is to dive into your emotions. Witness them so that you can identify them and move to a more logical perspective. The subsequent step is to identify what triggers these emotions. Ask yourself: Why are these emotions arising?

However, now I like to recommend veering far away from conventional EFT teachings. Instead, ask yourself: What subconscious core wounds created these triggers?

For example, Julie will notice that she has withdrawn because an emotional connection triggers her. Julie must then check out the core wound that triggers the withdrawal. In the Dismissive-Avoidant case, it is due to the many emotional neglects they experienced as a toddler and their belief that self-reliance is that the only way to self-preserve.

## Identify What Triggers Were Fired

How do you identify which of your triggers were activated? You want to identify which negative core belief you perceive was validated.

Ask yourself:

— What do I think this conflict means?
— What am I afraid will happen?

I have worked with thousands of clients that can distill their perceptions right down to painful core beliefs by taking the first step of asking such foundational questions. To help illustrate how these questions can reveal core wounds, consider the argument between the two sisters. Regarding using the car, Emily would ask: "What am I afraid will happen?"

The answer for the Anxious Attachment is: "My friends will leave me because I'm not fine." About her sister, her answer is: "I will lose an emotional reference to my sister due to this argument." As you can see, our perceptions are shaped by our core wounds or beliefs. These perceptions are projected onto arguments and make meaning for people that will not be understood or obvious to the person on the other side of the conflict. Without understanding core beliefs and the way they're triggered, communication in relationships becomes very difficult.

For Julie, the solution to "What do I think this conflict means?" would likely be: "My sister doesn't understand that my romantic relationship is in turmoil, which I'm expressing this caused pain. Vulnerability always leads to pain." The car's conflict triggered their core wounds in both their sisterly relationship and the relationships that are suffering from using the car. Without asking yourself these two key questions, the triggers that are being activated won't be revealed, and the conflict will be significantly more painful.

## Evaluate Your Level of Emotion

At this stage, it is important to gauge your emotional charge. Once you have witnessed your emotions and identified the underlying trigger that is contributing to your pain, ask yourself: On a scale from 7 to 70, 70 being most negative, how are my feelings? In traditional EFT, a person would be encouraged to watch their emotions for a period while they process them and settle down. Physiologically, their brain would shift back to higher processes, and their reptilian brain would deactivate. By also identifying the core subconscious wound that is present, you'll find proof of the other to start lessening the emotional charge related to the said trigger. For instance, Emily could remind herself of all the days that, despite her arguments with Julie, they made up once Julie had the chance to process her feelings. Julie could also find proof of the other by remembering whenever Emily supported her when she did share her feelings.

By examining the basis explanation for the situational pain from a reflective standpoint instead of a reactive standpoint, both sisters would gain the power to speak with each other more clearly about what they have. Once they are in a positively oriented headspace, they will find an answer together. In this case, it will be that Julie drops Emily off at the cottage before seeing her partner in the city.

At this point, what would be the emotional charge on the conflict for each of the sisters?

If you were in a similar conflict, what would you be feeling out of 10 now?

Keep in mind that it is essential to express your feelings once you feel approximately 5 out of 10 or less on an emotional scale since you are likely more misidentified from your emotions. At a six or above, an expression might not be conducive to finding an answer because you are still in a reactive headspace. You are still highly emotional, and your judgment is going to be clouded.

## Expressing Your Emotions

Research into the subconscious has discovered that the brain is in an almost hypnotic state for roughly the first seven years of life. In the infancy years, the brain produces mostly alpha and theta brainwaves while awake—the same brain waves produced under hypnosis.

As a result, in childhood, we are essentially human sponges for information. The young mind has enormous learning capacity and is deeply impacted by many aspects of its environment. In this era, we have many critical experiences that shape our Weltanschauung and perception of life.

One of these critical sets of experiences is what we study conflict. Conflict is a part of the human experience. It is inevitable and is usually a gorgeous opportunity for growth when handled appropriately. Yet, our earliest experiences of conflict are often quite painful.

Imagine Liam, a five-year-old who is filled with life and curiosity. One day, Liam is playing outside in his yard and thinks to go ask his neighbor across the road to play with him. Liam is inspired by this exciting notion and jumps up to go running across the road. He isn't brooding about cars passing, and fear is totally absent from his mind.

Just as Liam goes running across the road, his mother yanks him backward by his shirt and yells at him. His mother was terrified while watching him plan to meet the road without trying to find cars and was petrified by the thought that something awful could have happened if she wasn't there to prevent him.

Liam, on the other hand, feels extreme disappointment and frustration toward his mother. One moment he was having the time of his life, and the next, he was being yelled at and pulled around aggressively. He feels that she doesn't understand his innocence. He didn't mean to do anything wrong. He is helpless to elucidate himself, and when he tries to say himself to his mother, she isn't listening. Liam experiences shame, sadness, and helplessness at this moment.

This is one example of many of Liam's childhood experiences because it is for many individuals growing up. Parents discipline their kids because they are trying to keep them safe, but it often doesn't go well. Often, the parent's pain and worry get lost in translation and seem harsh, punishing, or shaming to the kid.

Two key factors are responsible for programming the subconscious: repetition and emotion.

As a result, our very suggestible subconscious minds tend to associate conflict with shame, helplessness, sadness, feeling misunderstood, and other painful feelings. The more times an experience is repeated, the deeper our programming will become. The more emotional an experience is, the more intense the programming also will become. These two factors create a challenging dynamic, as most of our childhood is spent in the socialization process.

How many times do you think Liam experienced moments like that with his mother? He experienced being reprimanded when he wanted to steer down the steps before he was sufficiently old. He experienced punishment when he tried to place his hands on the stove when it had been hot. Almost a day throughout childhood, Liam was on the receiving end of some kind of reprimand or anger.

This is how most people grew up, which means most of the subconscious associations about conflict are quite painful. In Liam's adult life, he is likely to be still carrying many of those same programs unless he has done extensive work to beat them. Liam's mind says conflict equals punishment and shaming.

Now let's fast-forward twenty years. Liam is now in a long-term relationship with his first girlfriend, Faith. Liam has a Dismissive-Avoidant attachment style, while his girlfriend Faith is Anxious.

One evening Liam forgets to call Faith back on his way home from work. He had a troublesome day at his new job and was preoccupied with his mind. When he arrives home, Faith is distressed. She expresses anxiety and frustration toward Liam for not contacting her. Immediately, Liam is experiencing Faith's emotions alongside all the stored associations in his own subconscious. Instead of having the ability to be present and hear Faith's feelings, his mind feels attacked and jumps at the need to guard and defend himself.

Liam raises his voice back at Faith. He tells her to go away and leave him alone that he had a stressful day. He isn't ready to validate her emotions and judges her for getting upset with him. He seems like she is shaming him and experiences resentment, sadness, helplessness. He also feels gravely misunderstood.

Liam's emotional response at this moment is a combination of emotions from things with Faith, alongside stored emotional associations rising from the past. The subconscious stores all memories and, as we all know, the emotional associations are still alive in those memories, waiting to surface.

Liam and Faith both struggle to speak, and it is sensible. They are both experiencing unresolved triggers that are stored subconsciously.

- How can they bypass this challenge?
- How can they convey with one another without triggering each other along the way?

First and foremost, it is important to acknowledge another important reason that arguments with our loved ones can cause a lot of pain. Most people think that we are arguing about being right versus being wrong. The reality is, we are nearly always arguing about being seen, heard, and understood by our loved ones. It is painful to feel as if someone you are in love with doesn't understand you in the heat of the moment. It often seems like we are disconnected, and typically that is what hurts more than anything.

This is where a gorgeous initiative comes in. it is possible to validate an individual's feelings without validating their behavior. If Liam used this tool, he might tell Faith, "Hi, honey. I can see that you're hurting at the moment, and I pity that. However, I don't just like the way you are expressing it, and that I have able to listen better if you change your approach to become gentler."

Although this might sound sort of a small trick, it works wonders. The impact of having the ability to validate a loved one's emotions in the heat of the instant is profound. It completely removes the helplessness, feelings of being misunderstood, and feeling shamed. More importantly, it prevents the defense reaction from being tripped due to the stored subconscious associations around conflict. As a result, the individual on the receiving end of this statement will probably be calmed down rather than fired up.

If Faith used the right tools to speak with Liam, she would also express her anxiety and frustration more appropriately. As discussed in the CBT section of this book, most of the pain we experience in a situation is predicated on the subjective meaning we give to a situation against the target content of the experience itself. This is often why you would possibly see Faith react differently if a lover forgot to call her than if Liam forgot to call her back.

As Faith expects Liam to arrive home and feels the need to unload her emotions onto him, she needs to spot this meaning. It is then important for her to express that she is upset due to her interpretation of things and to share from that perspective.

She might say, "Liam, I do know you had a long day at work, but when you didn't call me back, I interpreted that to mean that you don't care about me, and it really hurt. I want you to be more conscious about this in the future and perhaps set a reminder on your phone."

Faith is following these steps:

— Identify the meaning you give to a situation.
— Express using the following:

"When

interpreted it to mean

gave to it), and that I felt

you experienced)."

- 3. Identify what you need from your beloved and the strategy they will use to better satisfy that requirement.
- 4. Express using the following:

"I need you to (insert what you need). You can do this by (insert the "how"/strategy they can use)."

This set of steps does four crucial things:

- Because it expresses what Faith's experience and interpretation are, it lowers the likelihood of Liam getting triggered. This depersonalization makes it highly unlikely that Liam's got to protect himself and his negative associations with conflict will be triggered.
- It allows Faith to precise from an area of vulnerability. She is presumed to be heard when she is vulnerable because people are naturally open and receptive to vulnerability. Just consider the way you naturally check out a puppy or a baby. Expressing from vulnerability also opens the human capacity to be present.

— Faith offers an answer to Liam. It is very easy to fall under the trap of expressing hurt without expressing how a beloved can make that hurt better. This often leaves the matter only partially solved, as sometimes the need for resolution is often ambiguous.
— Faith describes the "how" for Liam. It is common for couples to try to resolve challenges by projecting what they might need onto their partner and attempting to do that instead.

Let's pretend that Faith said to Liam that she needed to feel supported by him. Maybe Liam feels supported by Faith when she cooks him a meal. So, the day after an argument, he tries to do that for her to be supportive. When Faith expressed the need for support, she secretly wanted Liam to go with her and make her feel validated through words. She appreciates the meal but feels as if Liam "didn't try hard enough."

It is extremely common for couples to possess different interpretations about how their needs are often met by each other. This is often why the "how" is so important in the initiative. Although it might be nice if Faith and Liam could read each other's minds, that just isn't how it works.

These four steps should be your gold standard for communication. Take a while to practice them. Consider three or four different times you felt frustrated in conflict and put them through these steps. When you feel like you know the steps, just like the back of your hand, practice applying them to challenging situations in your life.

Active listening is also a crucial part of resolving conflict, so remember to allow your partner to communicate with you respectfully.

# Exploring Productive Ways to Respond: Diving Deeper

EFT falls into three phases:

- — Assess and de-escalate
- — Change events
- — Consolidate change

The first phase focuses on witnessing and uncovering the initial emotional trigger. Then, one must specialize in the way to effectively communicate this core wound or trigger. Last, communication must be effectively received for long-lasting change.

Individuals are consistently trapped in how their emotions make them feel, and they often forget how to answer others' emotions. An important concept to recollect from the previous section is that people rarely argue about being right or wrong; they are more often arguing about being seen and heard. People feel a lot of pain in intense conflict with those they care about because, when someone has a different perspective, our subconscious perceives it as our feelings being treated as invalid. This ultimately feeds conflict.

So, begin by validating the emotions of the one that is expressing them to you. However, keep in mind that there is a big difference between validating emotions and validating behavior. For instance, if Emily were to get angry in the argument and storm out of the space, her conduct would be hurtful and unproductive. To validate Emily's emotions but not her behavior, Julie should tell Emily: "I see that you are hurt, which has led to an outburst of emotion. I might wish to hear more about why you are feeling this manner, but you can't behave in such an explosive manner." this is often an extreme example of how emotions can be validated, while actions aren't.

## Reframing the Matter

To help validate a partner's emotions or loved one at a time where your personal emotions are running high, begin by reframing the matter. This practice is additionally referred to as cognitive reframing. Cognitive reframing is the process of actively or voluntarily shifting your perspective to look at a problem or situation from a more objective space.

According to management coach Carter McNamara, there are multiple ways in which this will be done. A couple of examples include shifting from passive to active and shifting from others to oneself. The previous is an action-oriented approach that empowers the individual attempting to reframe things. For instance, Emily can reframe her thinking from "I will lose my emotional reference to Julie if we don't resolve this conflict immediately" to "What does Julie need immediately to feel like we can make up? What do I want right now? What steps can I take to find a compromise?"

The latter reframing approach involves viewing yourself from another perspective entirely. For instance, Julie can reframe her perspective from "Emily doesn't support me" to "What can I do to support myself immediately?" By partaking in cognitive reframing, both sisters will be better equipped to reflect on how they are feeling and how they will communicate these needs to their siblings. They are going to be better prepared to listen to their sibling's feelings and constructively answer them. It is also helpful if a verbal shift occurs. Use connective language like "together," "we," and "us" so that the conscious mind shifts out of an area of feeling defensive.

## Acceptance

Next, specialize in acceptance.

- — In what ways do you need acceptance from the person you are experiencing conflict with?
- — In what ways are you able to accept them?

To understand how to reach a compromise and ultimately acceptance, start with what attachment style you and the other person involved in this situation have.

To illustrate what this will look like, recall Julie and Emily. Transparency in the case of an Anxious Attachment is important. Since they tend to be people-pleasing, it is imperative that they do not sacrifice their needs that they convey them properly. If not, the Anxious individual will begin to harbor resentment. For Emily, this means communicating to Julie that she must talk things through because she feels she is in danger of losing her emotional connection to her sister.

However, she must also accept that Julie may need a little more time than she does to speak through the conflict. On the other hand, Julie must communicate that she needs time to process her emotions and accept that she may need to do that more quickly to be considerate of how Emily feels. Ultimately, this means both sisters express how they are triggered and need to accept and consider both their own needs and their sibling's.

It is also important to create a transparent, coherent strategy for the expressed and accepted requirements.

Since each individual's perceptions are uniquely shaped over time, saying "I need support" may mean various things to different people. Therefore, Emily must communicate to Julie that in the future, she may feel like she has an emotional connection to her sister, which can include Julie lending her the family car when she cares about her friendships. It also may include acts like getting dinner together to discuss their lives and talking more frequently.

On the day they are not together, Julie should communicate to Emily that she needs time alone to read and pursue the items she enjoys independently. In the end, the goal is to have both parties hear each other's feelings, validate each other's and their feelings, and express themselves in a way that permits them to compromise and set boundaries in which they will operate.

To conclude, Julie and Emily's story, imagine that they followed all of the steps described in this chapter. When Emily got mad at Julie and stormed out of the space, she paused and witnessed her emotions—where they're in her body—and labeled what she was feeling. Then, she asked herself: "What am I afraid will happen here?" Her response was: "That I will lose the emotional reference to my sister and friends." This led her to understand that she felt this way because of her core wound, according to her Anxious attachment style, was triggered: the fear of abandonment due to her inconsistent parenting.

Then, she would evaluate her emotional level by recognizing the trigger and witnessing it, and she or he will feel less pain related to things because she is best prepared to navigate it. By expressing this to Julie, she will be prepared to seek out a compromise for things at hand. Given that Julie follows the same approach, both sisters will have communicated what they are feeling and why they feel it. They will both be more empathetic toward the other's circumstances and more willing to seek a solution—instead of yelling and not talking to each other.

By combining EFT and attachment theory and using the results-oriented techniques I have distilled, Julie and Emily will come to an answer that is better for themselves and their relationships. Now, apply these steps to a conflict you are experiencing to make a significant change.

# Conclusion

Thanks once again, time for getting this awesome guide – "***Attachment Style***."

Let's hope it had been informative and able to provide you with all of the tools you would like to realize your goals, whatever they are.

At this point, you ought to have a way better understanding of what it means to be attached, especially in a romantic setting. You might have found yourself in love with someone who isn't healthily attached, or you feel you do not think that you can create healthy attachments. Hopefully, this book has provided you with a point of clarity that you can use to work out what it'll deem you to be happier and healthier in your relationships.

You were given a good range of information designed to help you study the most common attachment styles and how those styles tend to influence every aspect of your life. Hopefully, as you read, you began to acknowledge the reality of the matter—that your childhood will directly influence your adulthood. However, you ought to also recognize that your attachment style isn't fixed at all times. You can change it. You can do better. You can learn more. You can become better generally.

All that is left for you to do is make it a point to use the knowledge you have received. Put it to work — learn about what you can do to better yourself. Find out how you can bond more with your partner and the way, regardless of the design of attachment that you have developed, you can find true love. Don't feel like you are stuck in your relationships, with no recourse to do better. You will learn to have a far better, healthier relationship, and this book has given you everything you will need to determine this.

Thank you once again, time for taking the time to read through this book. Hopefully, it gave you everything you needed to start out gaining closure in your relationship so that you can begin to feel better in general.

*To your success,*